INDIA'S
SOCIAL HERITAGE

INDIA'S
SOCIAL HERITAGE

By

L. S. S. O'MALLEY
C.I.E., I.C.S. *retired*

LONDON · CURZON PRESS
NEW YORK · OCTAGON BOOKS

First published 1934
by the Clarendon Press · Oxford

Authorized reprint published by
Curzon Press Ltd · London and Dublin
and
Octagon Books · New York
A DIVISION OF FARRAR, STRAUS AND GIROUX INC.

1975

ISBN
UK 0 7007 0045 5
US 0 374 96147 6

Printed in Great Britain
by Kingprint Limited · Richmond · Surrey

PREFACE

SIR HENRY MAINE has pointed out in *Ancient Law* that one peculiarity which invariably distinguishes the infancy of society is that men are regarded and treated not as individuals, but as members of a particular group: a primitive society has for its units not individuals, but groups of men related by the reality or fiction of blood relationship. The social system of India retains many features characteristic of an early stage of social growth. Society is still largely communal in the sense that it is organized in groups. Individual life is based on collective standards and has to be in harmony with the life of the group. A man is not so much an independent individual as a unit in a group, to whose interests his own are subordinate, and the social organism may be described as a synthesis of groups rather than of persons. The groups are of several different kinds. Tribes, numbering many millions, still survive. Village communities have preserved their vitality from remote ages. Every Hindu who does not belong to a tribe is a member of a caste which has its own place in the social order. The joint family system, under which property is owned jointly by the group composing the family and not separately by its individual members, is the basis of Hindu law.

This little book is intended merely to give a simple statement of the principal features of the social system of India, which it is hoped may be of some service to those interested in its problems and may help to awaken interest in others.

My grateful thanks are due to Sir Benjamin Lindsay, Reader in Indian Law in the University of Oxford, for help generously given.

L. S. S. O'M.

CONTENTS

I

CASTE

THE most peculiar of the social institutions of India[1] is the caste system. It is peculiar in the sense that it is confined to India and is found nowhere else in the world. It is peculiar because of the extreme social segmentation which it produces; it is also peculiar because it is not a purely social system but is so closely interwoven with Hinduism as to have certain religious elements. Each member of the Hindu community belongs to one or other of over 2,000 castes, which divide it into groups arranged in a complex system of social differentiation. As between its members, a caste is a bond of union, but the system splits up society into sections which, owing to the prohibitions not only against inter-marriage, but also against eating, drinking, and even smoking together, prevent social fusion more perhaps than any other institution in the world. The caste system thus at once unites and divides thousands of groups, but its salient feature is mutual exclusiveness, for each caste regards other castes as separate communities with which it has no concern. The system does not however preclude association for common purposes or social intercourse, for subject to the restrictions which it imposes on mutual hospitality and matrimonial connexions, members of different castes may be on terms of intimacy or even friendship.

The caste system is the antithesis of the principle that all men are equal, for there is a hierarchy of castes, based on the principle that men neither are nor can be equal. The different castes rank as high or low according to the degree of honour in which they are held by the Hindu community

[1] Burma has been excluded from the purview of this book as it has neither ethnical nor social affinity to India proper.

as a whole, subject to the pre-eminence of the Brahman, who forms, as it were, the apex of a pyramid in which other castes are superimposed in layers, one upon another. A man belongs to, and, except in rare cases, remains till death in, the caste in which he is born. The social position of each individual is fixed by heredity and not by personal qualifications and material considerations. Differences of status are justified by the religious doctrines of *Karma* and the transmigration of souls. *Karma*, which many Hindus regard as the central doctrine of their religion, is briefly the belief that a man reaps as he sows, that he benefits by good deeds and is doomed to suffer as a consequence of evil deeds. According to his actions in one life, he is rewarded or punished in another by being born in a higher or lower sphere. In this life he pays the penalty or receives the reward for his acts in a former existence. If a man is a Brahman, it is because he deserves a high status as a reward for previous good deeds; if he is born in a low caste, it is because a previous evil life made a lowly estate inevitable. A man's caste is, therefore, determined by his past. It is his birthright by the working of an eternal and inexorable law.

For the low caste man the belief may seem to be shadowed by the gloom of predestination, but (assuming he is educated enough to know the philosophy of his religion) his life is not without hope, for he has the prospect of rising to a higher state in the next. Though his caste is fixed unalterably in this life, he may be reborn in a higher caste as a reward for righteous conduct and faithful performance of duty. From this point of view a man may be said to be master of his fate. His duty is defined as being, not (as in the Church of England catechism) in that state of life into which it shall please God to call him, but in that state of life in which he is born.

The number of castes is not immutable. Fresh castes come into being from time to time owing to the operation of various causes, such as the adoption of different occupations or occasionally of a religious cult. Some castes are sectarian in origin, i.e. their members start as members of a sect and end as members of a caste. Owing to the pervasive influence of the caste system and its extraordinary absorptive powers, more than one sect which originally sought emancipation from caste has itself become a caste. The Lingayat sect, for example, which arose in the twelfth century, had as one of its objects the abolition of caste distinctions; besides this, it was so imbued with the spirit of reform that it repudiated the practice of infant marriage and allowed the marriage of widows. By the seventeenth century the sect had reintroduced caste divisions, and had split up into sections which allowed no intermarriage. The Lingayats, who are mainly found in West India, where they number $1\frac{1}{2}$ millions, no longer belong to a single casteless community but recognize various groups, of which the highest claims the status of Brahmans while the status of others varies according to the castes of their ancestors. They still deny the religious supremacy of Brahmans, but they are not singular in this respect, for certain artisan castes in Madras also contend that there is no need for the religious services of Brahmans and themselves claim the status of Brahmans.

To come to more modern times, the creation of a new caste has only recently been brought to notice in the columns of *The Times*. The regiment of the Indian Army known as the Queen's Own Sappers and Miners, which was lately disbanded, used to recruit its men from among the Pariahs (Paraiyans) and Indian Christians of Madras; and we are told that among the Pariahs, from whom the sappers were drawn, 'there is growing up a special superior caste known as Quinsap, namely those who have served and are descended from those who have served in the Queen's Own Sappers and Miners.'[1]

Caste, though of great antiquity, was an institution unknown to the Aryans when they conquered and settled in the north of

[1] 'The Last of a Great Army', *The Times* of 20 October 1932.

India. They were a united community and the line of cleavage was not among themselves, but between them and the earlier inhabitants whom they fought and overcame. These former occupants of the country were mainly the people known as Dravidians, a dark-skinned race not without civilization, who were held in contempt by their fair-skinned conquerors. This, however, did not prevent the latter from taking their women as wives and mistresses, much in the same way as early European settlers in North America hated Red Indians but had Red Indian women as squaws. The Aryan dominion spread partly by direct conquest, partly by fusion with the non-Aryans, some of whom were driven to the recesses of the hills, while others were subjugated and assimilated. So far from waging a war of extermination the Aryans formed alliances with non-Aryans whose power made them formidable, converted them to Hinduism, and admitted them to their ranks. This is a process which has continued down to modern times, for it is a well-known fact that among the Rajputs, who represent the Kshattriyas (the fighting men of the Aryans), there are many descendants of aboriginals whose fighting qualities entitled them to respect. The great majority of the Dravidians, however, were treated as a subject race. Some were reduced to the position of serfs or slaves; others were free men engaged in manual work and in handicrafts, from which the Aryans, animated by pride of race and position, withdrew. Anxious to preserve their racial purity, their culture, and their standards of living, the Aryans relegated to a lower status the children of mixed marriages and those who were engaged in base pursuits, and the latter adopted similar lines of social demarcation among themselves.

There were thus divisions based primarily on race and partly on occupation. To these was added a more subtle and lasting differentiation based on religious status. The last appears in the classification of society found in the Laws of

Manu. This is a Brahman work of comparatively late date—in its present form it is ascribed to between the second century B.C. and the second century A.D.—which is regarded by the Hindus as the highest authority on their social institutions and family law. According to this work there were four classes ranged in order of precedence, viz. Brahmans, an order of priests and law-givers, who represented the world of religion and learning; Kshattriyas, the fighting and ruling class; Vaisyas, who were engaged in commercial, agricultural, and pastoral pursuits; and Sudras, whose life was one of service to the other three classes and who also obtained a living by handicrafts.

These four classes were called *varnas*, a word meaning colour, which undoubtedly had racial implications. The distinction between the four was, however, not based on race, but partly on occupation, and partly on religion. The first three classes had a spiritual birthright which was denied to the Sudras. They were recognized as 'twice-born', i.e. they went through a ceremony of initiation at an early age which made them eligible for religious rites. It marked their assumption of religious duties like the Christian ceremony of confirmation, and its outward symbol was the wearing of the sacred thread, a strand of thread suspended from or looped over the shoulder. The Sudras had no such religious privilege and were from birth to death under a religious disability marking their inferior social status. Below these four classes again was a fifth class consisting of degraded races, such as that known as Chandal, which were regarded as completely outside the pale.

In the different orders various castes were included. The Brahmans were at once a *varna* and a caste; other *varnas* were collections of different castes. There was, however, nothing like the present multiplicity of castes. The existing system is the growth of centuries, as major divisions have split into minor divisions and castes have been divided and subdivided over and over again, and eventually become stereotyped. The continual process of segmentation is the result of many causes, such as racial, religious, and occupational distinctions, territorial distribution, and, to some extent also, the regulations made by Hindu kings on the advice of their Brahman councillors in different parts of India. The classification of the Laws of Manu has, however, not merely an antiquarian interest but a practical present-day importance because the Hindu community accepts it as the basis of social precedence, and it is impossible to explain many features of the caste system as now existing without reference to it. Different castes are recognized as being the descendants of one or other of the *varnas*; according to their descent they are classed as 'twice-born' or as Sudras; and the social residuum which did not rank as a *varna* is regarded as the original of the untouchables, who in Madras are consequently known as the Panchamas, meaning 'the fifth class'.

What makes the caste system so baffling to the understanding of a European inured to a different social order and a different rule of life is the want of uniformity in the practices which it allows and the extraordinary range of its sanctions and prohibitions. It governs such matters as diet; it lays down marriage laws; it regulates to some extent the actual means of livelihood. There is an almost bewildering variety of usages as the combined result of many factors. One is that some castes have traces of a tribal organization, which affects their marriage laws. Another is that physical geography affects customs, especially of diet, in different areas: fish, for example, is a popular dish in the land of great rivers like Bengal, where it is abundant and cheap, but is eschewed in places where it is scarce and dear. A third is the fact that a caste is largely an autonomous unit. Certain principles, especially those relating to religion, may be laid down by the Brahmans, but their application and the enunciation of others are left to the castes

themselves, and the castes often act in entire independence
both of the Brahmans and of one another.

Much also depends on the extent to which the different
castes follow Brahmanical teaching and observe the orthodox
tenets of Hinduism; and it must be remembered that many
of the lowest castes, though recognizing the great Hindu
deities, have animistic beliefs and worship gods and godlings
unknown to Brahmanism. In the great majority of cases their
religious rites are conducted by non-Brahmans; Brahmans
neither officiate at their domestic ceremonies nor act as their
religious preceptors; and they live in ignorance of Brahmanical
doctrines, whereas higher castes base their social code on the
Hindu scriptures. One caste, therefore, may eat or drink what
another may not; it may have rules of marriage which other
castes regard as anathema; its members may legitimately earn
their livelihood in ways which would lead to excommunication
from a more orthodox or more punctilious caste.

The caste system splits up society into a multitude of little
communities, for every caste, and almost every local unit of
a caste, has its own peculiar customs and internal regulations.
The differences are so many that at a cursory glance the
caste system appears to be a mass of inconsistencies, which
would almost seem to argue a want of system; but such a view
is merely a case of being unable to see the wood for the trees.
There are unifying principles underlying the differences of
detail. The caste system has a synthesis of its own, and follows
a general plan which is recognizable in all parts of the country.

The members of each caste believe that they are all descended from a common ancestor, who may have been either
a real or a mythical personage. The idea of kinship is, as
pointed out by Sir Herbert Risley, 'certainly the oldest and
perhaps the most enduring factor in the caste system and seems
to have supplied the framework and the motive principles of
the more modern restrictions based upon ceremonial usage

and community of occupation.'[1] It is probably on this account that the most important and the most rigid of the rules laid down by caste are those which are concerned with marriage. The principal rule is that of endogamy, under which the members of each caste must marry within, and may not marry outside, the caste. The internal organization of the caste is also determined by regulations as to marriage. It is subdivided into sub-castes, which again are further subdivided into groups, and both the sub-castes and these groups are delimited on matrimonial lines. The three bodies may be compared to concentric circles, the caste being an outer circle, the sub-caste an inner circle, and the nuclear matrimonial group the innermost circle. The sub-castes generally resemble the caste in being endogamous, for marriage to any one other than a member of the same sub-caste is unlawful. On the other hand the innermost group, which is known by various names (such as *gotra*, *got*, or *kul*), is exogamous. The members of each are, or believe themselves to be, descended in the male line from a common ancestor, and intermarriage between them is looked on as little short of incest, so that they are obliged to marry outside the group but within the sub-caste. In actual working this is not so complicated as it seems at first sight. A friend of mine trying to find out how the different members of a sub-caste in a village were related was at once given a simple but effective demonstration. As soon as they gathered what he wanted to know, the villagers arranged themselves in two groups, the spokesman for one of which explained that the men of one were all brothers, and the others were their relations-in-law.

The fission of castes into sub-castes is due to many causes. One of the most frequent is the adoption of different occupations: it is common, for example, for the members of a caste who sell an article to separate from, and claim superiority to, those who produce it. Differences of social customs are

[1] *Imperial Gazetteer of India* (1907), vol. i, p. 337.

another cause of division, e.g. those who prohibit the re-marriage of widows and those who permit it form separate sub-castes. Membership of different religious sects is a third line of demarcation. For instance, one sub-caste may be Vaishnava, i.e. Vishnu is the object of adoration, and will not intermarry with a Saiva sub-caste, which specially venerates Siva. Territorial distribution also operates in the same way, members of a caste who have different places of origin or present residence being grouped in distinct sub-castes. Difference of language is yet another barrier to union in some parts of Madras, where members of a caste who speak Tamil, Telugu, and Kanarese belong to as many different sub-castes.

The view has been advanced that endogamy being the true test of caste and the sub-caste being the smallest endogamous unit, it should be regarded as the true caste. The sub-castes are, however, united by the belief that they all have a common origin as well as by the fact that they belong to the corporation or community known as a caste. The rule requiring marriage within the sub-caste is, moreover, by no means as rigid and immutable at that prescribing marriage within the limits of the caste. One sub-caste may be fused in another, and the ban against marrying outside the sub-caste may be raised: in recent years marriages between members of different sub-castes have taken place in increasing numbers; but a man may not marry outside his caste.[1] In addition to all this, there can be no doubt that it is the caste which determines a man's relation to the rest of the world, and not the sub-caste, which merely determines his relations to members of his own caste.

The relative position of the different castes depends not on any authoritative order of precedence but on public opinion

[1] The marriage in 1933 between a son of Mr. Gandhi, who belongs to a trading caste, and a Brahman lady is regarded as absolutely revolutionary. Even in his case a purification ceremony had first to be performed so as to bestow upon the bridegroom a quasi-Brahmanhood.

as to whether they are high or low. It is based partly on traditional beliefs as to origin in one or other of the *varnas* of the
Laws of Manu, but more largely on ideas as to their relative
purity in a ceremonial, and not a physical, sense. The conception of purity and impurity is the key to many of the apparent
enigmas of the caste system, and Dr. Ketkar regards it as the
chief principle on which the system depends.

'The Brahman', he says, 'is at the top of society because he is
more pure and sacred than other castes, while Mahar and Paraiyan
are at the bottom because they are impure. Thus purity is the
pivot on which the entire system turns. Rank, social position,
economic condition have no direct effect on the gradation from
the standpoint of caste. . . . Caste in India is strong and rigid
because the ideas of the people regarding purity and pollution
are rigid.'[1]

The idea of relative purity and consequent social inequality
underlies the rules as to eating and drinking together. No one
may therefore eat or drink with a man of lower caste, and in
Northern India at any rate the same rule applies to sub-castes.
Sub-castes of equal status may eat and drink together, but
when one claims to be of higher rank than another, it often
marks its claim to superiority by refusing to share a meal with
any member of a lower sub-caste. In South India, however,
there appears to be no general ban on members of different
sub-castes within the same caste having meals in common.

There is a general stigma of impurity attaching to the lowest
castes. This manifests itself in various ways. A man of higher
caste may be polluted by physical contact with one of these
low-caste men, e.g. by accidentally brushing against one, and
ceremonial ablution is necessary to restore his purity: in other
words, he should bathe in cold water. On the Malabar coast
some castes are believed to emanate impurity to such an
extent that their approach within a certain distance causes

[1] S. V. Ketkar, *History of Caste*, vol. i (Ithaca, N.Y., 1909), pp. 121–2.

pollution; but this is only a local custom, which has weakened of late years. Those who cause pollution by contact with or proximity to the high castes are also held to be capable of polluting temples and are therefore denied admission to them. The capacity for contamination extends to other inanimate objects, such as culinary and drinking vessels. The touch of some castes pollutes brass vessels, that of others pottery. Brass may be scoured but an earthenware pot so polluted is beyond redemption. It is unfit for use and can only be destroyed.

Food is similarly liable to pollution and once polluted is unfit for consumption; some castes have such power of contamination that if one of them casts his shadow over food, a punctilious high-caste Hindu will throw it away. There are inhibitions of the same nature as regards the persons from whom water may be taken. In South India men of one caste will not take water from those of another, but there is not the same rigidity in North India, where certain low castes, despite their low degree, are distinguished as *jalacharanya*, i.e. water-giving castes, from whose hands higher castes may take water.

The rules as to pollution do not apply to all food. The greatest strictness is observed in regard to what is called *kachchhi* food, i.e. food boiled with water, such as rice, which is usually prepared in a man's own kitchen. The general rule about this is that it should only be cooked by and taken from the hands of one's own caste, or—an obvious line of safety—a Brahman. On this account those who can afford to do so employ Brahman cooks so as to minimize the risk of contaminated food. There is a compromise, dictated by common sense and convenience, in regard to what is called *pakki* (i.e. food cooked with *ghi* or butter clarified by boiling), which may be prepared and served by others. It is usually prepared by confectioners and sold in their stalls, and is in demand in

various forms for consumption on journeys. Its immunity
from risk of pollution is ascribed to the fact that *ghi* is a product of the sacred cow and is therefore in itself purifying in an
extraordinary degree. An *impasse* naturally arises if *ghi* loses its
virtue by being mixed with impure substances. What is described as a panic is said to have spread through Northern
India in 1887 in consequence of suspicions that *ghi* was being
adulterated, and again in 1917 the Hindu community in
Calcutta was moved to a state of great excitement and alarm
because *ghi* was being adulterated on a wholesale scale. The
excitement subsided only when Government had passed
emergency legislation to prevent and penalize adulteration,
and after the offenders had been dealt with by caste tribunals.
Two Brahmans were sentenced to fines and excommunication, one for three months, the other for two years; and the
heads of two firms were fined, one a lakh of rupees (then equal
to over £6,500) and the other a quarter of that amount, and
were put out of caste for two years.

The belief in the necessity for preserving ceremonial purity
is also responsible for the objection to men who belong to the
'twice-born' castes making journeys overseas to European
countries, for it is obviously difficult, if not impossible, to
maintain orthodox standards in regard to food and drink either
on board ship or in a foreign country where they have to be
supplied by non-Hindus. It was on this account that the Laws
of Manu forbade the higher castes to reside outside the land
of their birth, and this injunction is still observed by orthodox
circles. Persons who have travelled to England and elsewhere
may consequently be excommunicated on their return to India
and required to undergo a ceremony of purification before
they can be restored to caste communion, though this rule is
now often quietly ignored.

Considerations of purity and impurity enter into the estimation in which different occupations and means of livelihood

are held. Naturally, those which involve dirty or repulsive work, such as scavenging and washing, are regarded as impure and the castes which follow them as debased. Anything to do with dead bodies, whether human or animal, is held to be particularly degrading. When a death occurs in a house, the family is regarded as impure for a prescribed period, which ends with a ceremony of purification. Those who handle corpses for the purpose of cremation are regarded as the dregs of the population, and even the Brahmans who officiate at cremations rank below other Brahmans. The Chamar again, who skins dead animals and dresses their hides, is one of the lowest castes, and the Muchi, a cobbler who handles dressed leather, though superior to the Chamar, is also among the very low. The comparatively few Brahmans who, under the pressure of need or greed, either perform domestic ceremonies or work as family priests for impure castes are themselves held to be impure on that account. They have fallen from their high estate and though they still rank as Brahmans in the estimation of lower castes, even the latter look on them as low Brahmans, and their fellow Brahmans will not receive them in communion. Yet, such is the virtue of the ministrations of Brahmans that the low castes for which they work rank higher than castes which are unable to secure their services.

The ideas as to what are honourable and what are dishonourable occupations are so extraordinarily varied that they can be reduced to no common factor. One idea which is generally prevalent, and which has its roots in the remote past, is that industrial occupations and labourer's manual work are base pursuits. There is no conception of the dignity of labour in India. The higher castes despise manual work and consider it beneath their dignity. Those castes whose hereditary means of livelihood is some handicraft, such as carpentry, pottery-making, oil manufacture, blacksmith's work, &c., all come within the lower grades of castes. Neither Brahmans nor

Rajputs, many of whom are land-holders, may undertake the physical labour of cultivation: above all, they must not, however poor, drive the plough. To do so is derogatory to their high estate, and they must maintain themselves as gentleman farmers. And yet there are Brahmans in Orissa, called Mastan Brahmans, who work like any ordinary cultivator or field labourer and who have been described as 'half-naked peasants, struggling along under their baskets of yams, with a filthy little Brahmanical thread over their shoulder'.[1]

As a rule, each caste has the tradition of a common occupation, such as trade, agriculture, some handicraft, hunting, and fishing; and many of those which are called functional castes, chiefly the industrial castes, actually take their name from their traditional occupation. It is accordingly known as the hereditary occupation, and many members of the caste (and in some localities perhaps most) still adhere to it—a fact which accentuates its hereditary nature. It must not be assumed, however, that they are under any obligation, either express or implicit, to do so. Nowadays, the castes, especially in Northern India, commonly have many other occupations besides the traditional one, and sub-castes are often differentiated by them. Whatever may have been the case in the past, the idea that at the present day a man must pursue the traditional calling of his caste is erroneous, and it is a fallacy to suppose that if one knows a man's caste, one can tell what his profession, trade, or handicraft is.

As in countries where there is no idea of caste, a son is naturally brought up in and succeeds to his father's business, trade, or industry; but there is no actual necessity for him to do so. He is free to adopt another occupation provided that it is one which his caste-fellows regard as lawful and honourable. Occupations are constantly being changed; there is particularly a tendency for low castes to take up those which

[1] Sir W. W. Hunter, *Orissa* (1872), p. 238.

are followed by higher castes. What a man may not do is to
adopt an occupation which is held to be dishonourable or
debasing.

The Laws of Manu laid stress on the necessity for a differentiation of functions between the four *varnas*. Each was
to preserve its own. A higher class was not to debase itself by
undertaking the work done by a lower, and the lower was not
to encroach on the preserves of a higher; but in case of necessity
higher classes were at liberty to do work which normally should
be done by lower classes. One main object was undoubtedly
to maintain the Brahmans in a privileged position as a sacro-
sanct order with a monopoly of learning. This position they
long maintained, and under early Hindu rule they were like
the clergy of the Catholic Church in medieval times, who, as
Froude points out in *Times of Erasmus and Luther*, reigned
supreme over prince and peasant by the magic of sanctity, had
the monopoly of learning, and enjoyed the secular power which
learning, combined with sanctity and assisted by superstition,
can bestow.

But Hindu rule was swept away by the Muhammadan conquest. The Moghul empire was established over the greater
part of India, and the Brahmans, changing with the times,
engaged more and more in secular pursuits. Their means of
livelihood were mainly secular even in the Maratha empire,
the founder of which, Sivaji, seeking to rule on traditional
Hindu lines, and therefore cherishing cows, Brahmans, and
caste, organized the administration on the principles of the
Hindu scriptures; one of the high Ministers of State was
a Brahman, called a Sastri, who expounded Hindu law and
applied its maxims to government. A contemporary writer,
who was himself in the Maratha service, remarked:

'I conceive it to be erroneous to consider the Brahman in the light
of a mere ecclesiastic. Doubtless there was a time when this order
devoted themselves to the service of religion; but this period of

pristine purity is past, and at present the Brahman is indifferently a merchant, a banker, and a soldier.'[1]

The list of occupations now followed can be multiplied scores of times. The adoption of secular occupations (unless they are so degrading as to involve loss of caste) does not affect the sanctity of Brahmans. They are a sacred rather than a sacerdotal order and are not priests in the sense in which that word is often used, i.e. of officiating in temple worship. Some, it is true, are temple priests, but temple service is not regarded as the true function of Brahmans, and the temple priests are held in low esteem by their fellow Brahmans.

The same tendency to take up any occupation which is at once permissible and sufficient for a livelihood is observable among other castes and has been accelerated by the improvement of communications and the development of new industries in modern times. The general result is that, whatever may have been the case in ancient times, caste can no longer be said to determine occupation. It is a common experience that any given occupation which is connected by tradition or heredity with a particular caste is actually followed by many others. A typical experience is that of a man travelling by boat on one of the great Indian rivers who inquired about the castes of his boatmen and found that his eight men represented six different castes, and only one the hereditary caste of boatman.

The ultimate sanction of caste rules is excommunication. This is a form of complete social ostracism, which cuts off a man, and very often his family, from all communion with his fellow caste men. So long as he is excommunicated, he is an outcaste, prevented from taking meals, drinking, and smoking with his fellow caste men, and from receiving food or water

[1] *Illustrations of some Institutions of the Mahratta People*, by William Henry Tone, commanding a regiment of infantry in the service of the Peshwa, *Asiatic Annual Register*, Miscellaneous Tracts, 1798-9, p. 127.

at their hands. Members of his caste will not enter his house or assist him either in sickness or in health; and the ban is upheld by the Brahmans, barbers, and washermen, none of whom will give him their services. He is condemned to uncleanness in clothes and person; he is unable to get his sons and daughters married—a positive sin according to Hindu belief—and when he dies, he is deprived of the rites which are necessary to his salvation.

Permanent excommunication is, however, reserved for the gravest offences, and it is more usual for a man to be excommunicated temporarily. He may be excommunicated *pendente lite*, i.e. until the charge against him is decided by a caste tribunal. This is merely an *ad interim* step taken by his fellow caste men in self-defence, for if they remain in communion with him and he is eventually outcasted, they are liable to be excommunicated themselves. When the case has been heard, and the charge substantiated, a man can be excommunicated for a definite period or until he has undergone a ceremony of purification or performed some prescribed penance. At the end of the time, or after completion of the penance, he is readmitted to caste, his re-entry into communion being generally celebrated by a feast (at his expense), at which he again eats and drinks with his caste associates.

The high castes have rarely any organization for dealing with social offences. The community merely passes a tacit verdict and by common consent ceases to have anything to do with a man believed to be guilty of a breach of caste rules. This procedure is open to no objection when a man is a notorious offender and his guilt is patent, but it may operate unfairly in other cases, and the suspect has no redress, for there is no body to which he can appeal and before which he can establish his innocence.

The low castes, on the other hand, have a systematic organization which is effective in upholding their social code

and exercises a healthy influence in keeping up standards of
morality and decency, though it also operates to perpetuate
much that is irrational. Each sub-caste acts as an autonomous
unit and has machinery to enforce its unwritten law. The
controlling authority is of two types, which correspond to the
types of village government. Village communities, as explained in Chapter IV, are controlled in North India by councils of elders and in South India by village headmen. So too,
the caste governing body in North India is a council, called
the *panchayat*, which is representative of the sub-caste in any
given locality such as a village or group of villages, while in
South India authority is vested in a caste headman. Many
castes in North India also have headmen, but power is not
concentrated in them, e.g. in the council the headman is only
primus inter pares. The caste councils are sometimes convened *ad hoc* for the decision of a particular question, but are
generally permanent bodies, constituting at once a kind of
standing committee and a court of judicature.

In South India their place is taken by headmen, who usually
hold office by hereditary right. Each sub-caste has its headman, who decides disputes and adjudicates in cases concerning
the caste law. In some cases he is an independent authority,
passing orders on his own responsibility or after consultation
with an assistant or vice-headman. In others he calls and con-
sults a council of the leading householders of his sub-caste in
the village before making a decision. More important matters
are decided by a council composed of headmen drawn from a
number of the villages in the neighbourhood and presided over
by a chief-headman. Appeals lie to this body from the orders
of each village headman. In most castes there is a third, and
in some cases even a fourth, appellate council or court, so that
there is a regular gradation of appellate courts. A similar but
shorter series of appellate tribunals is found among some castes
in North India, but there the courts are composed not of

headmen but of representative elders of the villages included in their jurisdiction.

The caste councils in North India generally decide on the cases brought before them without reference to Brahmans. The latter are consulted only if a man is charged with a religious offence or if the appropriate penalty seems to be a religious penance. Otherwise the castes act in independence of the Brahmans, and are rather proud of their independence. It rests with the members of the caste itself to decide what its customs shall be, and to adjudicate when a man is charged with their breach or neglect. In South India, however, the castes are by no means so autonomous, for the religious directors or spiritual preceptors of families, who are known as Gurus, and who are sometimes Brahmans and sometimes non-Brahmans, can excommunicate and sanction the re-admission to caste of members of those families. Besides this, a Brahman Guru is a supreme court of appeal for certain castes which are sufficiently high in the social scale to have Brahmans to minister to them.

The matters mostly dealt with are breaches of the marriage laws, the adoption of prohibited occupations, indulgence in forbidden food and drink, and eating, drinking, or smoking with persons not in communion with the caste or sub-caste. Unchastity in women is promptly and severely dealt with, but cognizance is rarely taken of sexual irregularities by men provided they do not offend against regulations as to marriage or as to food, as in the case of a man eating or drinking with, or eating food prepared by, a mistress of low caste.

There is little formality about the trial of a man charged with a caste offence. He is questioned, witnesses are heard, and sentence is passed without any record of the proceedings. Extra-judicial methods are sometimes employed. Some low castes in Madras occasionally resort to ordeals as a test of the justice of a claim. Both parties go to the village temple, a short religious ceremony takes place, and each of them plunges his hand into boiling *ghi* (clarified butter). Oaths are also taken before the idol in a temple, except by Brahmans, who object to taking them. In order to support his case a man lays his hand on the head of his wife or child, swears to the truth of his case, and invokes terrible penalties on them if his oath is false.

The penalties inflicted on those who are found guilty vary greatly. Sometimes they are excommunicated, either permanently or temporarily. Sometimes they are fined or ordered to pay the cost of a common feast for members of the caste in the village. The fines go into a common fund, which is expended on common caste purposes such as feasts, the cost of vessels used at them, the relief of needy members of the community, &c. Summary justice is also, though more rarely, meted out by means of corporal punishment. The guilty man has a flogging or kicking on the spot; or he may be subjected to some humiliating punishment, such as being paraded through the village seated backwards on a donkey, with his face covered with lime and with half his head shaved.

The high castes are too refined for punishments of this kind and favour purifying ceremonies of a religious nature. The most important, which is reserved for serious derelictions, is that known as *panchagavya*, which consists of drinking or tasting a concoction of the five products of the sacred cow, viz. milk, curds, *ghi* (clarified butter), cow-dung, and cow's urine. A concession to weakness is nowadays sometimes made by substituting honey for the fifth of these: this less noxious mixture is called *panchamrita*, i.e. the nectar of five substances. The lower castes of Madras have a different ceremony, by which both the house and the family of the offender are purified. The walls are sprinkled with water and white-washed; the floors are scoured with a mixture of cow-dung and water. The family priest consecrates some water and sprinkles it over all the members of the family and over their house. Sometimes also he brands the culprit on the tongue with a gold needle.

A remarkable case of *panchagavya* on a wholesale scale occurred in 1922 after the Moplah rebellion. During that rebellion the Hindus of Malabar were for some time at the mercy of the Moplahs, fanatical Moslems, who were guilty of the worst excesses. They were killed in cold blood, their temples were desecrated, their houses were burnt, their women were outraged, and men were forcibly converted to Islam by the painful operation of circumcision. There were thousands of helpless victims, but their helplessness did not save them from being put outside the pale. Some Brahman authorities held that they could not be readmitted to the fold of Hinduism, but must remain outcastes, but eventually more merciful views prevailed and readmission was sanctioned by an assembly of Brahmans, on condition that they went through the following purifications and penances for their enforced fall from grace. Those men who, in order to save their lives, had repeated the Islamic confession of faith, those from whose heads the Moplahs had cut the tuft of hair which is a distinctive mark of a Hindu, and those women who had had their ears bored and been compelled to wear Moplah jackets had to undergo *panchagavya* for three days at a temple, to make such offerings as were within their means, and to repeat at least 3,000 times a day during those three days the sacred names of Vishnu or Siva according to their cult (Vaishnava or Saiva). The same series of expiations was prescribed for men who had been forcibly circumcised and for women who had been forced into cohabitation with Moplahs with one change, viz. that the divine names had to be repeated 12,000 times daily. A longer period of purification was prescribed for those who had been forced to eat food cooked by Moplahs. They had to observe the same ceremonies for forty-one days, during each of which the sacred names had to be recited 12,000 times, besides bathing in certain sacred water and obtaining a certificate to that effect from the temple authorities or from their family priests. For some other forced 'sins' the period of expiation was fixed at twenty-one days, with the repetition of the sacred names 12,000 times a day.

The caste system is unknown in Baluchistan and is of little importance in Sind, the North-West Frontier Province, and some parts of the Punjab, where tribal units predominate. In these areas the social organization is based on the tribe rather than on caste in the accepted meaning of the word.

'However caste as a religious institution may form the basis of society elsewhere, it is quite certain that amongst the agricultur-ists of the Punjab the basis is tribal divisions and subdivisions, and, below these, occupations. The Hindu agriculturist of the Punjab knows nothing of caste except as represented by the tribe. No doubt he respects the Brahman, and calls him and feeds him on occasions of rejoicing or sorrow, but he would never dream of referring to him or to the Hindu law for guidance in his daily life.'[1]

Throughout the Punjab the people are more independent of Brahmanical authority and more indifferent to the niceties of caste rules than Hindus in other parts of India. Here the two great agriculturist communities, the Rajputs and Jats, who number many millions, are organized on tribal lines, and though they have caste rules, do not observe the rule of endogamy which is generally characteristic of the caste system. They occasionally intermarry, the Rajputs, who have the higher status, taking Jat wives but refusing to marry their daughters to Jat husbands.[2] Within each community the prohibition against the intermarriage of different groups does

[1] C. A. Roe and H. A. B. Rattigan, *Tribal Law in the Punjab* (Lahore, 1895), p. 11.
[2] Tradition asserts that the Rajputs and Jats were originally of one stock, and that the Jats were reduced to a lower rank because they did not keep their women in seclusion and allowed their widows to marry again.

not exist as it does in a regular caste. Their marriages are subject to the contrary rule of exogamy, i.e. a man must take his wife from another group which may be called a clan, a sept, or a sub-caste according to the point of view.

Similar divergences from the ordinary caste system are found elsewhere among castes whose constitution is largely tribal. Kinloch Forbes wrote in *Ras-mala or Hindoo Annals of the Province of Goozerat*:

'The Rajpoots use animal food and spirituous liquors, both unclean to the last degree to their puritanic neighbours, and are scrupulous in the observance of only two rules—those which prohibit the slaughter of cows and the remarriage of widows. The clans are not forbidden to eat together or to intermarry and cannot be said in these respects to form separate castes.'[1]

The Marathas of Western India are another great community in which the rules of marriage resemble those in force among the Rajputs and Jats of the Punjab. They are divided into two classes, the Marathas and the Maratha Kunbis, and the Marathas, who claim to be the higher of the two, will marry Maratha Kunbi women but will not give their own women in marriage to them; they are also free from caste restrictions on eating together. The Kathis, who have given their name to the territory of Kathiawar, are another community subject to the rule of exogamy. They are divided into two sections called Sakhayat and Awartya, and a member of one must marry a member of the other. Their marriage law affects their agricultural economy, for the Sakhayat are landowners, and the Awartya are landless, and intermarriage serves to restore the balance between them.

The caste system is seen in its greatest rigour and precision in the south of India. Nowhere else are there such sharp divisions between the castes, such a carefully regulated graduation of social rank, and such a strict observance of the minutiae

[1] Loc. cit. H. Yule and A. C. Burnell, *Hobson-Jobson* (1903), p. 754.

of ceremonial rules. The system there is peculiar in more than one respect. The actual castes are unlike those of North India, for there is an almost complete absence of what may be called the middle castes, the representatives of the Kshattriyas and Vaisyas. The castes there fall into three main groups, viz. the Brahmans, who are a class apart, the Sudra castes, and the Panchamas, the last of whom are more generally known to the English public as untouchables or depressed classes.

A number of the castes belong to one or other of two great factions called Right-hand and Left-hand, a division unknown in any other part of India. The Right-hand faction consists mainly of cultivating and trading castes, the Left-hand of industrial castes. The schism dates back many centuries, and its origin is unknown and merely a matter of conjecture. One theory is that it originated in a revolt by artisan castes against Brahman domination and was connected with the struggle between Jainism and Brahmanism, the former religion, which was stronger in urban areas, finding adherents in the artisan class, which was largely urban, while the latter was upheld by the conservative cultivators. Certain it is that the artisan castes, who lead the Left-hand faction, deny the supremacy of Brahmans, call themselves Viswa Brahmans, and wear the sacred thread. The two factions are bitterly hostile. Their quarrels seem to be rather like those of the 'big-endians' and 'small-endians' of *Gulliver's Travels*, being concerned merely with questions of precedence and ceremonial detail. In the past the faction fights, in which thousands might be engaged, used to be so serious and productive of such bloodshed that at times the combatants had to be dispersed by artillery; and though outbreaks on this scale no longer occur, the fanaticism of the factions is always a potential danger.

The caste system has infected to some extent the social system of the lower classes of Moslems, though it is utterly at variance with the precepts and traditions of Islam. As is

well-known, Islam is a religious brotherhood, a fellowship of
believers, in which distinctions of race and class should be
abolished according to the teaching of the Prophet, who declared 'Great and small, noble and plebeian shall be equal
among you'. A Moslem may marry, eat, drink, and worship
with any other Moslem, whether prince or peasant; but many
Moslems of the lower classes have little knowledge of the tenets
of their religion. Living among Hindus, they have assimilated
many of their religious and social ideas, join with them in
Hindu festivals, and base their own social system on conceptions of caste, so that there is the anomaly of caste distinctions
existing within the fold of an essentially casteless religion.
There are many functional Moslem groups whose occupations,
transmitted from generation to generation, have given rise to
divisions of the same character as among the Hindu castes.
There are, for example, communities of weavers, oil-pressers,
washermen, and barbers, each of which imposes restrictions
exactly as if it was a caste, forbidding its members to marry,
eat, or drink with members of another group. Like castes these
groups have councils to try offenders against their rules, and
they may outcaste a man who takes a wife from an inferior
group and degrade him and his children to the inferior group.
    Pride of descent and social position also separate classes.

'As the twice-born Aryan is to the mass of Hindus, so is the
Mohammedan of alleged Persian, Afghan or Moghal origin to the
rank and file of his co-religionists, although now, since many
descendants of converts from Hinduism have by education and
position sprung to the fore, they too are receiving more honour
than formerly and are even sought after for marriage with
daughters of foreign extraction.'[1]

Saiyids again have objections to women of their families marrying Sheikhs, though they will take wives from the latter, whom
they raise to their own level. There are, further, two main

[1] J. Talke, 'Islam in Bengal', *The Moslem World* (1914), pp. 12-13.

social groups called Ashraf and Ajlaf, and as a rule a member of the former will not willingly give his daughter in marriage to a man of the latter; but it would be a mistake to suppose that this has anything to do with the conception of caste. The names of these two groups mean noble and low respectively, and the division between them is like that between aristocrats and plebeians and that which used to exist between the upper and lower classes in Europe.

The persistence of caste prejudices has before now created difficult problems in the Indian Christian community, converts objecting to sitting in church with converts drawn from lower castes and to taking the communion with them; not very many years ago there was actually a case in the law courts in which a section of an Indian congregation which maintained caste exclusiveness contested a ruling of their Bishop forbidding them the exclusive use of part of a church.[1] In South India the oldest Christian Church, the Syrian Church, was organized socially on caste lines. The Syrian Christians, who at one time had their own chieftains, were treated by their Hindu neighbours as constituting a caste of good status, for they were held to be equal to the Nairs. They themselves were proud of their high estate, avoided intercourse with the lowest castes, and, refusing to admit them to fellowship, made no effort to convert them.

Caste distinctions have also been recognized by Roman Catholic Missions in South India. The great Jesuit missionary Robert de Nobili, who laboured there in the early part of the seventeenth century, feeling that he could only hope to convert high caste Hindus by abstaining from an attack on the system, treated it as a social and not a religious institution and sanctioned the retention of many caste usages, including that of untouchability. When the Mission which he founded extended its work to the lower castes, it was divided into two

[1] *The Indian Year Book for* 1924, p. 312.

branches, one of which devoted itself to the conversion of Brahmans, while the other concentrated on the depressed classes. The priests attached to each branch adapted themselves to the customs of the communities among which they worked. The missionaries with Brahman converts assumed the status of Brahmans and would not minister to the untouchables nor enter their churches, chapels, or houses; the other missionaries had nothing to do with the Brahmans. Priests of the two branches held aloof from each other just as if they themselves were Brahmans and untouchables.

'One missioner would be seen moving about on horseback or in a palanquin, eating rice dressed by Brahmans, and saluting no one as he went along: another, covered with rags, walked on foot, surrounded by beggars, and prostrated himself as his brother missioner passed, covering his mouth lest his breath should infect the teacher of the great.'[1]

The Mission founded by de Nobili flourished for a time and claimed over two million converts, but difficulties arose as the number of missionaries working among the depressed classes was insufficient for their needs and the higher order of priests could not minister to them except in secret. The Jesuit method of compromising with and actually countenancing Hindu customs was condemned by non-Jesuits, and eventually a Papal decree was issued in 1704 directing *inter alia* that the priests of the Brahman converts should visit untouchables when ill and give the sacred unction without distinction of caste.

Roman Catholic Missions still continued, however, to tolerate and make allowances for caste distinctions among their converts in South India. The Bishop of Madura wrote in 1862:

'Doubtless the distinction of castes is here carried to a ridiculous and often unreasonable extreme; but to aim at destroying it

[1] The Rev. W. Strickland, S. J., and T. W. M. Marshall, *Catholic Missions in Southern India to 1865* (1865), pp. 57–8.

abruptly, to seek to confound all ranks and conditions, and to make an onslaught on that which immemorial usage has consecrated, would be to excite revolution in the country, to injure the interests of religion instead of serving them, and to enter on an idle pursuit of a result which could never be reached. Prudence suggests—reserving altogether its approbation for distinctions legitimate in themselves and indispensable for public order—that we should tolerate what does not contradict the ordinances of the Church until the progress of time and the development of sound notions shall introduce the reforms which good sense demands.'[1]

The passage of time has not yet made it possible to dispense altogether with caste separatism, at any rate in regard to the depressed classes. Accordingly converts who are descendants of untouchables may be separated from converts of higher origin by means of partition walls or railings down the aisle, and there may even be churches at either end of a village for members of the two communities. Trouble arises when attempts are made to introduce a change: not many years ago in a village where a new pastor wanted his congregation to sit together in church, the Christians of higher caste seceded and reverted to Hinduism; but on the other hand some of the Christian depressed classes in South India are beginning to resent such discrimination and have joined a movement, called 'the self-respect movement', which aims at abolishing social differences.

For the last hundred years the Protestant missions, with one exception (the Leipzig Missionary Society in South India), have steadily refused to countenance caste among their converts. Bishop Heber was inclined to treat it as only a distinction of rank and to hold that just as gentlefolk in English country churches at that time took the Sacrament apart from the lower classes, so Indians of higher caste might communicate apart from members of the depressed classes. But a firm

[1] Loc. cit. Rev. W. Strickland, S.J., and T. W. M. Marshall, *Catholic Missions in Southern India to 1865* (1865), pp. 224–5.

stand was made against it by Bishop Daniel Wilson, on the ground that in South India it had caused divisions which were incompatible with the spirit of Christianity. Different castes would not take communion together, Sudras had precedence of Pariahs at the communion table, and Pariahs not only sat apart in the churches while alive but were buried apart when dead. He ruled in 1833 that the distinction of caste must be abandoned decidedly, immediately, and finally. So wedded were the people to their old ways that this order caused 'something like a revolution in the Church in South India'. One Sudra congregation renounced its membership in a body; hundreds of catechists resigned; petitions and memorials were submitted to the Government of India, one of which may be quoted as typical of the view of the higher castes, for it stated, ungrammatically but emphatically, their objection to eating in communion with 'Pariahs as lives ugly, handling dead men, drinking rack[1] and toddy, sweeping the streets, mean fellows altogether.'[2]

Other Missions followed the lead given by the Church of England on the ground that caste is not merely a class distinction but to a great extent a religious institution which is irreconcilable with the idea of Christian brotherhood. To the abolition of caste distinctions must be attributed, in part at least, the enormous increase in the number of converts drawn from the depressed classes, who are admitted to fraternity with converts from higher castes and live in unity with them in the common life of the Christian Church. In spite, however, of the teaching of Protestant missionaries caste separatism persists among their converts in some parts, notably in South India, where the depressed classes present a problem of special

[1] Arrack.
[2] Eyre Chatterton, *History of the Church of England in India* (1924), p. 165; J. Richter, *History of Missions in India* (1908), pp. 169–70; G. O. Trevelyan, *Life and Letters of Lord Macaulay* (1884), p. 272.

difficulty. According to the Madras Census Report of 1931 caste prejudices are present everywhere in some degree, though they are not so strong among Protestants as among Roman Catholics, who have more converts of higher caste. Social equality is so far from being realized that it is no more possible for a Christian whose caste was originally Vellala to marry any one who comes from the depressed classes than it would be for a Hindu Vellala to contract such a marriage, and boycott would be as sure a consequence. The Census Superintendent concludes that though there is something to be said for the existence of castes as social units within the Church, the continuance of violent prejudice and social stigma is another matter, and one which cannot tend to strength and self-respect within a Christian community.[1]

[1] *Madras Census Report for* 1931, Part I, p. 328.

II

THE DEPRESSED CLASSES

THE term 'depressed classes', which is used to describe the lowest Hindu castes, has a wider significance than the term 'untouchables', which is also applied to them. The latter is descriptive of one of the incidents of their position, viz. that a Hindu of any caste higher than theirs must have no contact with them because he would thereby contract ceremonial pollution, which, according to orthodox belief, must be removed by ceremonial purification. The epithet depressed, however, connotes more. It covers not only low status in the hierarchy of caste combined with religious and social disabilities, but also a low economic condition.

The depressed classes have also been called the outcastes (or the outcaste Hindus) and the Pariah castes, but neither of these names is altogether apt. They are certainly not outcastes in the sense of having no caste, for they are divided into many different castes and observe caste distinctions as rigidly as their social betters. Pariah castes is an obsolete term and particularly unsuitable from an Indian point of view, for Pariah is an Anglicized form of the name (Paraiyan) of one only of the many untouchable castes found in South India and nowhere else. The depressed classes are also known in the south of India as Panchamas, i.e. the fifth class, the other four being the four *varnas* of the Laws of Manu mentioned in Chapter I; but this name, which has replaced that of Pariah castes, is only a local designation which has not been adopted elsewhere. Harijan and Antyaja are names which have been applied to them by Indians in recent years; some of them have assumed the designations of Adi-Hindu and Adi-Dravida; and at the census of 1931 they were classified officially as 'the exterior castes'.

So far from being homogeneous, the depressed classes are

as disparate as the higher castes. There are similar gradations
of rank, and social distinctions are as sharp among them. The
rules as to intermarriage and eating and drinking together are
equally strict, if not stricter. There is even what is called 'untouchability within untouchability', i.e. the higher untouchables can be polluted by contact with lower untouchables. The
former, while feeling their inferiority to higher castes, have
equal pride in their superiority to those which rank below
them, an equal contempt for them, and an equal fear of falling
to their level.

By origin many, if not most, are descendants of ancient
occupants of the land, chiefly the races known as Dravidian,
though there is also a pre-Dravidian strain. In the north of
India the higher classes were absorbed into Hinduism by their
Aryan conquerors and, if of good fighting quality, given the
status of Kshattriyas, but no such good fortune came in the
way of the masses, who were treated as a subject people. To
them were assigned menial tasks, from which their proud
supplanters held aloof.

The same explanation cannot be given of the origin of the
depressed classes in South India. There was no Aryan conquest in that region, though there was an infiltration of
Brahmanical beliefs and customs among the Dravidian population, which had a culture of its own. It has been suggested
that those who first adopted the social organization introduced
by the Brahmans became Sudras, and that those who originally
remained outside it, but were eventually brought into it by
the force of example and the spread of Brahmanical influence,
became the lowest stratum of Hindu society. Some, however,
are the descendants of tribes of pre-Dravidian origin; practically all the primitive tribes south of the Godavari are said
to have become depressed castes.[1]

Most of the depressed classes obtain their livelihood by

[1] *Census of India Report for* 1931, Part I, p. 507.

labour, chiefly agricultural. A minority are artisans, village servants, and small cultivators. Each village contains a certain number on whom devolves the necessary but disagreeable work of the cremation of the dead, scavenging, and skinning the carcasses of animals, all impure occupations, which account for the low esteem in which they are held. No such reason can be assigned for the treatment of others who simply suffer from a hereditary stigma. At the same time it must be admitted, even by those who sympathize with them, that there is much in the manner of life of a large proportion of this unfortunate class which causes feelings of disgust among Hindus of higher caste and more refined habits. A report of the Telugu Mission, which is infused with sympathy for them, says: 'It is true that naturally the Panchamas are poor, dirty, ignorant, and, as a consequence of many centuries of oppression, peculiarly addicted to the more mean and servile vices.'[1] Many eat carrion. What this means may be gathered from the account of an eyewitness, who saw 'a group of degraded creatures sitting round a crimson heap. It was the carcase of an animal that had died by the road, which they were tearing in pieces for a meal. At a little distance, kept off by angry shouts, was a circle of scavenger dogs, waiting greedily for what should be left.'[2] The eating of carrion is, in the opinion of the Bombay Depressed Classes and Aboriginal Tribes Committee, one of the most important causes of their being kept down in the world; but it is a congenial diet to many, who would object to giving it up. Recognizing this, the Committee has actually recommended legislation forbidding the practice when the leaders of the depressed classes in any particular area consider that the majority would willingly accept the restriction. The fact that local option is appended as a condition to the recommendation is significant.

[1] Loc. cit. Sir V. Chirol, *Indian Unrest* (1910), pp. 180–1.
[2] W. E. S. Holland, *The Goal of India* (1918), p. 160.

Again, a large number are a drinking class, fond of intoxicants and prone to intemperance, habits which are held by
the temperate orthodox Hindu in abhorrence. There is no
doubt that an unduly large part of their earnings goes to the
liquor shops, and this is one reason for their general poverty.
Thriftlessness is another; but the main reason is that by custom
and the working of the caste system they are tied to low paid
labour. They are debarred from many occupations owing to
their supposed polluting qualities; their traditional callings
yield little more than a subsistence; and except in Eastern
India most are poor, and some desperately poor.

Owing to their low level of subsistence, their improvidence,
and their reckless expenditure on domestic ceremonies—a
trait which they have in common with higher castes—they
are as a rule heavily indebted. Many live in perpetual debt,
which increases their subordination to their employers and the
village money-lenders. For want of real property they may
pledge their labour as security and even be reduced to a state
almost of bondmanship. A labourer may take a small loan
and in return bind himself to work for his creditor for life, or
for ninety or a hundred years, or until the loan is repaid.
Compound interest is added to capital, the debt is never liqui-
dated, and the interest is taken out in lifelong work. In some
parts the son is considered liable for the debt when his father
dies; elsewhere he is not liable, but when he grows up, he may
take a loan like his father and execute a similar agreement.

In parts of Bihar, where this system used to prevail, those
who entered into such agreements were more like farm servants than serfs, for they were given their food, a house to
live in, and also a small monthly pittance. Their lot was not
therefore so hard as it might appear, for it was to the interest
of their master to keep them fit for work, and they had their
food in times of scarcity as well as of plenty. If a master
neglected this duty, the bondsman was *ipso facto* released from

his bond and at liberty to leave his service. But, while he discharged it, they could never better their lot by going elsewhere. They were not free men, and though they were never destitute, they were a lean and hungry lot. In Bihar and Orissa, where they were known as *kamias*, bondmanship of this kind has been made illegal since 1920 by a measure entitled the Kamiauti Agreements Act, which prevents agricultural labourers from binding themselves or their families under any circumstances to work for a particular master at a particular wage for longer than one year. In Madras the practice appears to linger, for according to an official report, 'in many districts the Panchama field labourer is so tied up by debt to his master (who takes care that the debt shall not be redeemed) that he is practically in the position of a serf. The system of manmortgage by which a labourer binds himself and frequently his heirs to service till the debt is redeemed is well known.'[1]

Educationally, the depressed classes are on as low a level as they are economically: the census of 1931 has shown that only 3 per cent. are literate. The reason lies partly in the difficulties about schools, which will be mentioned shortly, partly in their own indifference to education. A labourer or small cultivator wants his sons to help him as soon as his help is of any use and is unwilling to keep him at school. But they are capable of higher things. The Telugu Mission report already cited states:

'Where they are able to escape their surroundings, they prove themselves in no way inferior, either in mental or moral character, to the best of their fellow country-men. . . . In many schools and colleges Christian lads of Panchama origin are holding their own with, and in not a few cases are actually outstripping, their Brahman competitors.'

Some, who have been ordained as clergymen of the Church of England, have added knowledge of Greek and Hebrew to knowledge both of their own language and of English. Others

[1] Loc. cit. W. S. Hunt, *India's Outcastes: A New Era* (1924), p. 39.

have risen in secular professions, and the present leader of the
depressed classes, Dr. Ambedkar, a Mahar by caste, who has
been a Delegate to the Round Table Conference, has distinguished himself in the sphere of politics.

They have also rendered good service in the army, especially
those known as Mazbi Sikhs, who are well known for their
fighting qualities. They are the descendants of sweepers who
have accepted the Sikh religion and given up the degrading
functions of their ancestors. The first to be admitted as Sikhs
were three sweepers who rescued and brought back from
Delhi the body of the martyred Guru, Tegh Bahadur. A body
of them was recruited for service in the siege of Delhi during
the Mutiny, when Neville Chamberlain said that their courage
amounted to utter recklessness of life. Eight of them carried
powder-bags and their lives in their hands under Horne and
Salkeld when the Kashmir gate was blown up, and their names
are inscribed on the arch to this day. The Mazbi Sikhs serve
in Sikh Pioneer regiments and are not enlisted in the other
Sikh class regiments, as Sikhs of higher class generally refuse
to serve with them.

Till recently the depressed classes of Madras and Bombay
were eligible for the Bombay and Madras Corps of Pioneers,
but these corps have been disbanded. A writer in *The Times*,
lamenting their abolition, has described how the depressed
classes and Indian Christians from whom they were largely
drawn 'with rum and beef in their bellies and Brown Bess on
their shoulders, carried the Union Jack from the Great Wall
of China to Africa and the French Islands'.[1] The stoppage of
recruitment is a loss to the depressed classes, for not only did
the army provide an attractive opening for them, but they rose
to commissioned rank, and many officers on retirement were
appointed honorary magistrates and helped to raise the prestige
of their community.

[1] 'Last of a Great Army', *The Times*, 20 October 1932.

According to the census of 1931 the depressed classes, or as they are called by the Census Commissioner, the 'exterior castes', aggregate nearly 50 millions, of whom 40 millions are found in British India—a number nearly equal to the total population of Great Britain—and the remainder in the States. Different criteria have from time to time been applied in estimating their numerical strength, with the result that the estimates differ by many millions. In arriving at the figure of 50 millions the disabilities taken into consideration were five, viz. (1) obstacles in the way of using public institutions or amenities, such as schools, wells, or bathing places; (2) prohibition on entry into Hindu temples or, in some cases, on the use of burning *ghats* (i.e. places of cremation); (3) refusing to render them service on caste grounds, e.g. by barbers, tailors, or washermen; (4) refusal to take water from them; and (5) pollution by contact or proximity.

These constitute a formidable list of disabilities, but they do not all apply to the depressed classes in all parts of the country. They are treated much better, for instance, in the north of India than in the south. In Assam they are freely admitted to schools, and there is no discrimination about the use of wells. In the Punjab untouchability is not held to mean, as elsewhere, that pollution is caused by contact—only actual scavengers are untouchable in this sense—but that high caste Hindus cannot touch food cooked by the castes in question. These castes, moreover, though not allowed to enter the richer Hindu temples, are not debarred from minor temples. In the United Provinces an orthodox Hindu cannot take food or water from those classed as untouchables; strict religious usage requires him to purify himself by bathing after contact with one of them; custom in many cases prevents them from using the village well; and it is often found that though untouchable boys may be admitted to the village school, they are isolated there. The same description applies generally to Bihar and Orissa. In Bengal a high-caste Hindu who preserves orthodoxy will not allow an untouchable to touch his person, food, or drink, or to sit on the same seat (except in trains); in Eastern Bengal there is a saying that if a man is in a narrow lane with houses on either side belonging to Sunris (a caste of liquor vendors), and an elephant comes along it, he should let himself be trampled underfoot by the elephant rather than enter one of them.

In Bombay the social and economic disabilities of the depressed classes in rural areas, as described by a committee of inquiry appointed by the Bombay Government, are deplorable.

'As a degraded people the depressed classes are expected to follow a code of behaviour according to which the depressed class man may not do anything which will raise him above his appointed station in life. He should not dress in a style superior to that of his status, nor should his wife adorn herself with ornaments after the fashion of the higher-class Hindu women. He should not have a house better or bigger than the houses of other people in the village. He should not own land or be independent. He should not take to new and more remunerative services except those which are customary. It is true that some members of the depressed classes have risen above the low status prescribed by custom for them, and have acquired property, high place, and even social esteem. But for the majority this particular attitude of the orthodox Hindu has been responsible for keeping them in their servile condition.'[1]

The conditions in the south of India are much the same as in the Bombay Presidency, but in Malabar and Travancore the refinement of unapproachability has been added to that of untouchability. In other words, a Brahman can be polluted by their mere proximity as well as by contact. The depressed classes are held to emanate impurity and so convey a kind of

[1] *Report of the Depressed Classes and Aboriginal Tribes Committee, Bombay Presidency* (Bombay, 1930), pp. 3–4.

atmospheric pollution. In some parts they are still expected to cover the mouth with the hand when addressing a Brahman so as to prevent their breath reaching him, very much like Job when he said: 'Behold, I am vile. I will lay mine hand upon my mouth.' In Malabar and Travancore a scale of distances, ranging from 8 yards to 32 yards, is laid down within which certain castes may not approach a Brahman. Members of these castes may not pass along some roads frequented by Brahmans. Others they may use, but they should give the Brahman warning of their presence by shouting out (like a leper in the Middle Ages), and they should leave the road when he draws near and get to the necessary distance in the fields even if they are under water. This practice, however, is local, and it must not be imagined that it is general.

Except in South India the general rule is that untouchability applies only to personal contact, and in orthodox circles this is an attribute of Europeans and other non-Hindus. It may even be extended to articles touched by them. In Manipur in Assam, if a European so much as sets foot on the plinth of a verandah, the whole house will be abandoned, and Colonel Alban Wilson tells us that a Manipuri will not touch anything simultaneously with a non-Hindu: 'if you pay him money, he expects you to drop it into his hand, and if he passes you a polo stick, he chucks it so that you must catch it.'[1] In some places, however, if an untouchable becomes a Christian, he loses the attributes of untouchability or unapproachability, though this is not the case in others, such as Travancore. In Gujarat also and in some parts of the Deccan Indian Christians who used to belong to the depressed classes, or are descended from them, and who still live in the same quarters, share their disabilities such as exclusion from the village well or school. It has also to be recorded that in spite of their religious tenets both Christians and Moslems in some parts of the Bombay

[1] *Sport and Service in Assam and elsewhere* (1924), p. 126.

Presidency are so affected by the caste prejudices of their Hindu neighbours that they too treat the depressed classes as untouchable.

In the villages immemorial custom requires the depressed classes to live in separate hamlets or blocks of houses outside the village proper. In Berar the quarters of the Mahars, who are the village menials, have a strip of white or red rag flying over them to warn people of high caste against inadvertently going too near them. Their quarters are as a rule sordid and insanitary; very often they are near the village midden or the place where the carcasses of cattle are dumped. In some areas postmen refuse to deliver letters at their houses, despite the rule requiring personal delivery, but hand them to a third person to deliver, and it is not uncommon for Hindu under-lings in Government and other public offices to refuse to hand them a paper or take one from their hands.

Incidents such as these are mere pin-pricks in comparison with their treatment as regards the use of wells and admission to schools in some areas. They suffer under disabilities which they are seldom able to get over owing to the opposition of their caste superiors. They are not only in a minority, but have neither wealth nor influence to help them in asserting themselves. If they do so, they often have to face persecution and boycott, e.g. masters will not employ them, shopkeepers will not sell to them, the money-lender will not give them loans, and if they have land, their neighbours' cattle may be driven on to it and their crops destroyed.

There is no difficulty about the water-supply if they have separate wells or if there is a flowing river or a large reservoir (known in India as a tank) from which they can draw water at a place apart from those used by their neighbours of higher caste. The difficulty is acute if their wells dry up or if they are dependent on common village wells. In that case they may have to go miles for water or depend on good-natured villagers of higher caste pouring some of the water which they have drawn for themselves into their pots. It is scarcely necessary to dilate on the consequent inconvenience and even hardship which they suffer, for they must have water for drinking, cooking, and bathing: even during the famine of 1919–20 the Deccan Marathas refused to allow the untouchable Mahars to use the village wells when their own had dried up, and they had to wait and collect what muddy liquid trickled past after the cattle had been watered.

The problem, however, is by no means easy to solve. Orders may be passed that they are to be given access to wells, but they are negatived by the opposition of the higher castes, as may be seen from the experience of Bombay. In 1923 the Bombay Legislative Council passed a resolution that 'the untouchable classes be allowed to use all public watering places, wells and *dharamsalas* [rest houses] which are built and maintained from public funds, and are administered by bodies appointed by Government or created by Statute, as well as public schools, courts, offices and dispensaries'. The Bombay Government passed orders implementing this resolution so far as it related to public places and institutions belonging to and maintained by Government. The local bodies were divided in opinion, some voting for acceptance of the resolution, others against it: a few first accepted it and then rescinded their acceptance.

'But', it is reported, 'whatever the nature of the resolution the result has been the same. We have not been able to find a single instance where the depressed classes are using continuously the same public well as the higher classes. There may be such wells, but if so, they must form an infinitesimal proportion of the public wells of the Presidency.'[1]

The reason for the failure was simply the stand made by the higher-caste Hindus. The depressed classes as a rule were too

[1] *Report of the Depressed Classes and Aboriginal Tribes Committee, Bombay Presidency* (Bombay, 1930), p. 52.

timid to assert a claim to the use of a public well; in the few cases where they did so, they gained little or nothing. Either the orthodox Hindus gave up using the well to which the depressed classes resorted, so that the latter merely got an additional well, or by means of boycott they compelled the depressed classes to give up using it. It should be added that the depressed classes themselves are not free from reproach in regard to the use of wells. They have, as already stated, higher and lower castes, and the higher object to the lower drawing water from their wells on the ground that they would be polluted—another instance of 'untouchability within untouchability'.

The education of the depressed classes is a problem of equal magnitude. Their children have a right to be admitted to public schools, but if they exercise it, the schools may be boycotted by the parents of higher caste who withdraw their children, or the depressed classes may be boycotted till they withdraw their own. In some cases, however, the educational authorities have successfully held out against a boycott of the schools, carrying on with the children of the depressed classes as the only pupils until the others give in and send back their children. In some parts, moreover, there is not the same prejudice: in the Bombay Presidency, for example, the depressed classes are admitted to most of the schools, though they are debarred from them when they are held in temples, which they would pollute by their presence.

Even when they are admitted, there is apt to be discrimination against them. In many schools they may not sit in the same classes with other children, but are kept apart in some dark corner, or banished to the verandah; besides which the teachers may refuse to give them books or paper or take them from their hands. In extreme cases they may be altogether excluded from the building and made to sit outside. When this happens, they naturally do not attend regularly in the rainy season, and for the rest of the year are dependent on what they can hear through the open doors and windows, unless the teacher from time to time leans out of the window to give them intermittent individual instruction. These difficulties disappear where there are separate schools for the depressed classes, but these schools emphasize and perpetuate the cleavage of classes. They are also below the standard of the common schools, owing to the lack of interest taken in them by the depressed classes themselves, who are not yet fully alive to the value of education and see no advantage in keeping their sons at schools when old enough to earn money or help their parents.

In spite of this indifference and the handicap caused by the active opposition of the upper classes, there has been a great advance, for the number of boys of the depressed classes at school was quadrupled in the twelve years ending in 1929. There has, moreover, been a marked improvement in other directions. In cities and towns untouchability is now far less in evidence. The depressed classes mix freely with others in the streets and markets and have no trouble in getting houses unless they have risen in the world and want to rent a house in a good quarter from a conservative landlord. Railway travel and more recently the advent of the motor-bus have done much to break down untouchability. Their economic position has changed for the better, especially in Western India. This is due partly to the fact that, being willing to turn their hands to practically anything, they have taken advantage of the opportunities offered by new industries, as for instance motorcar driving, in which they have taken part without any objection being raised; it is also due in part to their educational progress which has qualified them for more profitable employment. On the other hand, they suffer as a community from an inferiority complex—a spirit of humility and of shrinking subordination—which, combined with poverty and ignorance, are a bar to general progress.

Action to ensure equality of treatment for the depressed classes has been taken by the Governments of Baroda, Mysore, Bombay, and Madras, areas in which the problem is most acute. A measure passed some years ago in Baroda provided that the depressed classes were not to be prevented from taking drinking water from any well: any village which broke this rule was to be punished by withdrawing Government contributions to it. In the same State a compulsory Education Act imposed an obligation on the depressed classes in common with the upper classes to send their children to school, and any school which refused them admission could have its grant withheld. In Mysore an enlightened policy has been followed by the Maharaja, and administrative measures have been taken for the social betterment of this unfortunate community. Members of it have been given seats in the State Representative Assembly; State schools have been opened to them and special scholarships provided for them; they have also been settled in healthier quarters and in some cases provided with land.

In the session of 1929–30 the Madras Legislative Council passed an Act which enabled all classes, irrespective of caste or creed, to have access to, and the use of, all public places, such as streets, markets, and water reservoirs maintained from municipal funds, and penalized any obstruction to their use; an Act with similar provisions was passed subsequently by the Legislative Council of the Central Provinces on the motion of a leader of the depressed classes. The Madras Government also insists on their admission to publicly-managed schools and makes it a condition of grants to others. In February 1933 the Government of Bombay issued instructions that in hospitals and dispensaries maintained by Government no distinction should be made in the treatment of patients belonging to the depressed classes. At the same time it laid down that applications by local bodies for the assignment of Government land for wells and reservoirs were not to be granted except on the condition that all castes would have equality in their use, and that grants to local bodies for village wells, water reservoirs, and rest-houses might be reduced if they did not secure equality of treatment.

These measures are the outcome of an extraordinary change in the attitude of a large section of the Hindu community. At the beginning of this century many would have denied that the depressed classes belonged to the Hindu community, and would have maintained that they were completely outside the pale. This attitude has been abandoned partly for political and communal reasons, as Hindu politicians are only too anxious to have them classed as Hindu voters as a counter-weight to Moslems. Even more, however, the change is due to humanitarian and philanthropic influences, for which thanks are largely due to Christian Missions and the Salvation Army, which have worked for, and among, the depressed classes and shown what they are capable of; many millions have embraced Christianity and by doing so have, quite apart from religious regeneration, attained a new dignity of manhood. Nor should the Arya Samaj be overlooked in this connexion, for it has admitted the depressed classes in large numbers to its membership.

The leaders of Indian thought have taken up their cause and aroused the conscience of their countrymen by proclaiming that their treatment—man's inhumanity to man—is a reproach to India and a blot on its national life. They have not merely rendered lip-service but have fortified precept by practice. The Maharaja Gaekwar of Baroda gave a banquet in 1931 at which he and the leading officials of the State ate in company with the leaders of the depressed classes. As is well known, Mr. Gandhi himself has advocated their social claims for many years. He has adopted a girl of an untouchable caste as his daughter, and in his seminary (*asram*) no sweepers are kept,

Brahmans and others do menial sanitary work, and untouchables are admitted even into the kitchen. Various societies
have been established for their uplift, such as the Servants
of the Untouchables Society; mention should also be made
of the Servants of India, the members of which take a
vow to regard all Indians as brothers and to work for the
advancement of all without distinction of caste or creed. The
depressed classes, moved by the impact of education, have
begun to realize and resent the injustice of their hereditary
inferiority and the denial of their inherent rights as men. The
more advanced have begun to organize; associations for the
vindication of their cause have been started, such as the Madras
Depressed Classes Federation; and an all-India Conference of
the Depressed Classes has been held for some years. But the
movement is so far not general, for many of the depressed
classes, as the result of age-long subordination, have not the
spirit to rebel against an order of things which is declared to
be divinely ordained.

The energies of the leaders have been specially directed of
late years to securing a right of admission to temples from
which they are debarred by the Brahman custodians on the
ground that their presence would pollute the shrines. Their
tactics have been mainly those of peaceful siege of the en-
trances. The priests have in some cases erected barricades
against them, and the agitators for admission have waited at
the barricades week in and week out, in the hope that their
obduracy might wear down the obduracy of the priests: in one
case the depressed classes lay down every day for nine months
on a road outside a temple which they were besieging. Threats
have also been made that they or the advocates of their cause
would starve themselves to death unless the gates of some particular temple were opened to them. This is a form of *dharna*,
which is a criminal offence under the Indian Penal Code. It
applies pressure to enforce a claim or demand with the backing

of supernatural terror, for the implication is that if death results from starving, the death will lie at the door of the man who refuses to concede a demand.

The prolonged fast of Mr. Gandhi in 1932 in fulfilment of a similar threat has done more for the depressed classes than perhaps a century of agitation would have done. The occasion was the communal award which the British Government was forced to make in September 1932, because the Delegates to the Round Table Conference had failed to come to an agreement. This award provided that the depressed classes should vote in the general constituencies like other Hindus and also have special seats and constituencies because they were unlikely otherwise to secure adequate representation or to be in a position to safeguard their interests. It was accordingly provided that seventy-one special seats should be assigned to them for not more than twenty years, and that those seats should be filled by election from special constituencies in which only members of the depressed classes electorally qualified would be entitled to vote.[1] Mr. Gandhi took exception to this scheme on the ground that separate electorates for the depressed classes could 'simply vivisect and disrupt' Hinduism, and he declared that he would starve himself to death unless and until Government withdrew its scheme.

The Hindu community was electrified by his decision. Their leaders stepped into the breach and came to an agreement with the leaders of the depressed classes, by which the latter will have 148 seats reserved for them out of the general electorate seats in the provinces, and arrangements will be made for the primary election by the depressed classes of the candidates, who must belong to the depressed classes. Besides this, 18 per cent. of the seats allotted to the general electorate

[1] The seats were divided among the provinces except the Punjab, North-West Frontier Province, and Sind, where the depressed classes do not require special protection.

are to be reserved for the depressed classes. This agreement was accepted both by Government and by Mr. Gandhi on the seventh day of his fast.

Mr. Gandhi's fast had a purely political object, viz. to force the hand of Government on a constitutional question, but it had repercussions on the social and religious position of the depressed classes which were as unexpected as they must be welcome to all right-thinking men. The Hindu community was profoundly stirred. Many temples opened their doors to them for the first time. The Maharaja of Kashmir issued a proclamation that they should be admitted to State temples in his territory. The Chief of Bhor, a small State in the west of India, announced that untouchability in public places, such as courts and offices, was to be abolished. Higher castes fraternized with them at religious festivals. At their final session at Poona, the political leaders, after ratifying the agreement, passed a resolution that the social disabilities imposed on the depressed classes should be removed and that they should have free entry into temples. They supplemented this by appointing a committee to raise funds to educate public opinion by means of propaganda throughout India, especially in the villages, and an All-India Untouchability League was formed to further the cause.

But when the wave of emotional excitement had subsided, a reaction set in. The orthodox party organized opposition to the movement. Some temples which had been opened to the depressed classes were again shut against them; the higher castes refused to enter others on the ground that they had been polluted. In order to revive enthusiasm Mr. Gandhi undertook in May 1933 and successfully carried through another fast lasting twenty-one days, his motives being connected only with the cause of the depressed classes, and not with politics. The depressed classes seem to have had doubts as to the value of this fast, and also as to the results already achieved, if we may judge from a published statement of their leader, Dr. Ambedkar.

'I do not believe,' he said, 'that his fast will have any more effect on Hindu society in relation to untouchability than that of the temporary galvanization of a dead horse into activity. Hindu society does not think rationally about its conduct towards the depressed classes. It leads its customary life and is not prepared to relinquish it even at the bidding of Mr. Gandhi. It refuses to reassess its old values. As regards temple entry, the depressed classes all over India have made it clear to Mr. Gandhi that they will have nothing to do with it regarded as a final solution of the problem of removal of untouchability. They would accept it only if Mr. Gandhi would make it clear that it was the first step in a general reform of Hindu society involving the break-up of the caste system.'

In the meantime the leaders of the orthodox Hindu community continue to deny the depressed classes right of entry into temples and have declared that they will resist with all their might the abolition of caste distinctions in Hindu society and of what they call disciplinary regulations in temple worship.[1] The result of the struggle between them and the party of reform has still to be seen. At any rate the issue has become a live one for the whole of British India, for a private member's Bill has been introduced in the Legislative Assembly of which the scope is sufficiently described by its title, The Temple Entry Disabilities Removal Act, 1933.

If the Bill passes into law, it will be a great step forward, but the extent of its beneficial effects should not be over-estimated. The actual gain will not be so great as it might appear to Europeans accustomed to the congregational worship of one God. The Hindus have a multitudinous pantheon, and the temples over which Brahmans preside are dedicated

[1] Others besides the depressed classes are excluded from some temples in the south of India, to which only Hindus of high caste are admitted.

to the great gods and goddesses of Hinduism, such as Vishnu, Siva, and Kali. The name of other gods and godlings is legion; it is these which are the popular objects of worship, and many of them have no temples or Brahman priests. The general tendency of worship in South India has been lucidly described by Dr. R. Sewell:

'In the matter of religion the mass of the people in Southern India may be said to have been always Dravidian, Aryan Hinduism being a mere veneer. The great temples are of course dedicated to Aryan gods, but the people seldom visit them except on festival days. The religion of their daily life has always been, as it is at the present day, that of their forefathers; namely worship of local deities and of patron gods and goddesses, with propitiation of demons; praying to the former for temporal blessings and averting the anger of the latter by sacrifices and offerings.'[1]

This account applies to other parts of India as well as the south. The villagers do not often enter the temples of the great Hindu deities. They acknowledge that these are the sovereign deities of Hinduism to whom reverence must be paid. But their worship of them is only intermittent, for they feel that the lords of heaven are too high and mighty to trouble about their humble affairs. It is the minor deities, especially the village godlings, who in their belief are concerned with their daily life, chiefly as the source of trouble, and whom it is worth propitiating. The officiants who offer up sacrifices to them are not Brahmans; the ritual is not that of orthodox Hinduism. The great gods of the temples with their Brahman staff of priests consequently play a minor part in the religious life of the masses, including the depressed classes.

In any case there is no congregational worship in the temples such as there is in Christian churches, nor are they used for ceremonies such as marriages and funerals. The Hindus

[1] *Imperial Gazetteer of India* (1909), vol. ii, pp. 322–3.

offer their devotions at a shrine individually and not as a body, and they approach the gods through priests. The depressed classes may also make offerings, but may not be present when the latter present them but must remain outside the temple. There is perhaps a parallel in the position of the Proselytes of the Gate among the Jews, for they too were not allowed to enter the inner court of the Temple. What is really far more important is the family worship—the ceremonies at birth, marriage, and death—and this worship is conducted by Brahmans of a higher class than the temple priests. Domestic rites are more essential than temple ritual; family sacraments are more to be observed than sacrifice and oblation; and until it is recognized that Brahmans of the same class as perform these sacraments for the twice-born castes may do so for the depressed classes without prejudice to their status, the latter will not obtain religious equality. Such a consummation, however much it may be desired, is not likely to be attained speedily, for, both by Hindu scriptural law and by established custom, the depressed classes are not eligible for such sacraments. There are, it is true, already Brahmans who so far demean themselves as to perform priestly services for them, but these Brahmans sacrifice their own status by doing so, for they are regarded as mere hedge-priests, and not as true Brahmans, on the principle 'He that toucheth pitch shall be defiled'. In any case the removal of a religious disability does not entail the removal of social disabilities. Religious equality does not involve social equality, and the right of temple entry does not affect social status, which is determined by the general feeling of other castes. It is for this reason that the leaders of the depressed classes regard the right of admission to temples as one part only of the problem, while some of the depressed classes themselves regard the question of their economic betterment as of more practical importance. A Hindu gentleman who gave evidence before the Joint Select Committee on

Indian Constitutional Reform stated recently that his own experience in a constituency which he represented was that the depressed classes were uninterested in the question of temple entry. For four years he had tried to get them admitted to temples, but he found that they themselves said: 'We want food and clothing. Give us food and clothing; we do not want temples. What we want is cheaper food and cheaper clothing. We have got our own temples and are quite satisfied.'

III

FRONTIER TRIBES

THE tribal system plays a minor but still an important part in the social organization of India. Tribes numbering nearly 25 millions are found in the Himalayas, the country adjoining them, and the hilly tracts of the interior. They fall into three main groups according to their geographical distribution in the north-west, the north-east, and the interior, and they belong to different racial stocks, viz. Indo-Afghan or Indo-Iranian, Mongoloid or Tibeto-Burman, and Dravidian or pre-Dravidian. Three religions, Islam, Hinduism, and Animism, are represented among them, and they are in different stages of civilization, for some are nomads, others are still semi-nomadic, while others have become organized communities of settled agriculturists; but all alike have certain features characteristic of communities which are still in the tribal stage.

Along the north-west frontier is a congeries of tribes, believed to number three millions, to which the term Pathan is generically applied. The term is a linguistic one meaning a man who speaks Pakhtu or Pashtu, and the tribes themselves are distinguished by different names, such as Yusufzais, Orakzais, Mohmands, Afridis, Mahsuds, and Wazirs. The great majority are inhabitants of the mountainous country lying beyond the North-West Frontier, which is known variously as tribal territory or trans-border territory or independent territory.[1] Each of the tribes is, or claims to be,

---

[1] India has two boundary lines. The first is an inner line, known as the administrative border; this is the boundary line of the settled districts of the North-West Frontier Province and consequently of British India. The second is an outer line known as the Durand line after Sir Mortimer Durand, who settled it in 1893 after negotiations with the Amir of Afghanistan; this is the boundary between the Indian Empire and Afghanistan. Between the two is the tribal territory, which, though part of India, is not

descended from a common ancestor. It is split up into clans, and the clans are subdivided into septs claiming agnatic kinship. Attached to the tribes are groups of dependants known as *hamsayah*, i.e. dwellers beneath the same shade. These consist of families who have left one tribe and sought the protection of another, and of various dependants of alien extraction, such as traders, artisans, and menials, who are attached to, but not members of, the tribes.

Some tribes north of the Kabul river are loosely united under great chiefs, but most of them, especially those in the south, such as the Afridis and Wazirs, are intensely democratic in spirit and acknowledge no master. Some tribes have *khan khels*, i.e. sections from which chiefs are chosen, but the chief, when there is one, seldom has any real power. He comes to the front as a leader in war and on freebooting raids, but the Pathan with his fiercely independent character is loath to admit that any man is his superior and boasts that he serves as an equal. The real authority and such government as there is are vested in the *jirga*, i.e. a tribal assembly or council of elders of the clans or septs composing the tribe, who meet to discuss common tribal affairs. The characteristic institution of the Pathan tribes appears in fact to be not chieftainship but the headship of *maliks* or elders meeting in council. It is they who administer the tribal law, but the extent of their authority is limited by the fact that the Pathan prefers to take the law into his own hands.

Social justice is based on the idea of retribution, and in the absence of a centralized government with power to impose sentences and carry them into execution, it is left to the injured party to exact redress. In the Swat Valley, however, tribal councils have sufficient authority to hold trials and inflict punishments extending to the death penalty. Though the

directly administered by the Government, though a certain measure of control is exercised in some areas.

general idea is that private wrongs may be redressed by private vengeance, the right of reprisal is to some extent modified and restricted by the payment of pecuniary compensation for personal wrongs. Damages are paid for injuries and blood-money for murder, the life of a man being valued at double that of a woman. The law of the border is *lex talionis*, 'an eye for an eye, and a tooth for a tooth', or fair damages for both, and justice is enforced by personal action, so that the right of private war is recognized. Murder in retaliation for murder is both an act of justice and a social duty, and long continued blood-feuds perpetuate the state of private war. The trans-frontier Pathans, in fact, lead a gladiatorial life, and 'a well-aimed bullet is more effective than any consideration of right and justice'.[1]

Blood-feuds mostly originate in disputes about women, land, rights of irrigation, and inheritance of property. Quarrels about women are a particularly common cause of prolonged vendettas and lead to such a series of murders as—to quote from Mr. Steevens's *In India*—shooting the man who stole your wife, or shooting the man who shot your brother who stole his wife, or shooting the man who shot your father who shot his brother who stole your mother! Some feuds are settled by the mediation of the *jirgas*; others yield to no compromise but are a heritage of hate passing from generation to generation till the original cause of the quarrel is sometimes forgotten. They are suspended sometimes by common consent: a truce is called when it suits both parties, as at the seasons of ploughing, sowing, and harvesting. They are kept in abeyance when the tribes make common cause in a war against the British, and also when the parties serve in the Indian Army. Happily also what may be 'a truce of God' reigns in the Khyber Pass owing to the recognized convention that there must be no shooting on or along the sides of the road running through

[1] *India in 1929–30* (Calcutta, 1931), p. 39.

it. The lay-out of the villages and the construction of houses are determined by this internecine strife. Only the strong man armed may keep his life and his goods in peace. Villages are surrounded by high walls, and contain towers 30 to 50 feet high, which are at once watch-towers and peels; the base is an almost solid mass of stone and the door of entrance is 15 to 20 feet high and is reached by a ladder, which is drawn up when night falls. Fields within its range of fire can be cultivated; beyond that is a danger zone.

The recognition of the vendetta as a solemn duty naturally limits social intercourse, but on the other hand hospitality is as essential a part of the Pathan's code of honour. His readiness to give shelter and protection to the stranger is at times embarrassing to the civil authorities in the border districts of British India, for sanctuary is given to criminals who have fled from the neighbouring districts, so that the hills become a refuge for outlaws. This hospitality has its limits. The Pathan is a curious mixture of courage and cruelty, treachery and good fellowship; and the guest, whose safety is inviolate so long as he is in the house, may be stabbed in the back as soon as he is outside the village lands.

A meagre sustenance is wrung from the hard stony soil of the mountain valleys and slopes, and is supplemented by forays into British districts. Brigandage is due not merely to age-long traditions of lawlessness and restless savagery, but also to the reaction of economic causes on people whose means of subsistence are uncertain and sometimes insufficient. During these raids they carry off cattle, any money they can find, and villagers whom they hold to ransom:[1] incidentally they kill and wound those who oppose them. These raids are inseparable from the state of society which has existed among

[1] A world-famous case of kidnapping with a view to ransom occurred in 1923, when Miss Ellis was carried off from Kohat and rescued by the efforts of Mrs. Starr and two Indian officers.

the tribes for many centuries. The history of this region so far
back as it is known is one of robber bands and raiders, war and
pillage. The words of Lord Dalhousie are still as true as when
he wrote some eighty years ago: 'They have been murderers
and plunderers since the days of Ishmael, their father; and
it is not to be expected in reason that they should at once be
converted to order and harmlessness merely because British
rule has been advanced to the foot of their mountain fast-
nesses.'

Each tribe, and within the tribe each clan, occupies a well-
defined tract, within which the families cluster in villages
surrounded by the lands which they cultivate. The tribal
system extends to the tenure of land, which is in the joint
ownership of the tribe or clan and is divided into shares held
by its members. They have no right of individual ownership,
but merely a right to share in the common property of the
tribe. By old tribal custom it is periodically redistributed
among the different members of the tribe, as used to be the
case among the Irish septs; in some cases not only the land,
but also rights in irrigation and even houses are redistributed
so as to restore equality. Sometimes the distribution is confined to adult males, sometimes it is made according to
'mouths', i.e. every one, male and female, old and young
(including even the child in the womb), has a right to an equal
share. Among the Marwats of Bannu, who in 1905 had a
redistribution among 'mouths' to the number of 2,000, every
man took time by the forelock and some years beforehand
married as many wives as he could, thus increasing the birth-
rate and the area of his holding. After this the Marwats
abandoned the custom of redistribution. It has also been
given up in the Swat valley, because it was found to be
fatal to improvement. In the latter area, where houses as
well as land were redistributed once in a generation, men,
knowing that they might not reap the fruits of their labour,

would not even plant a tree, much less refurbish their houses.[1]

The right to a share in the common land is sometimes a criterion of membership of a tribe. In Swat and Dir the name Pathan is applied only to a man having such a share, which carries with it the right to take part in village and tribal councils: conversely a man who loses his share forfeits the name of Pathan and a voice in council.[2]

Society is organized on a patriarchal basis, descent and inheritance being in the male life. The position of women may be realized from a statement made in Mr. Thorburn's *Settlement Report of the Bannu District*.

'Most of our wildest tribes scorn the idea of a woman having any rights in property; they tell you that she is as much a chattel as a cow, and if she, when widowed, wishes to retain any interest in her husband's property, she must marry his brother; and that a man to be entitled to hold his share of land must be able-bodied. Our courts do not uphold such customs.'[3]

The Baloch, or, as they are commonly called, the Baluchis, have some points in common with the trans-frontier Pathans, for they too are divided among tribes, which are subdivided into clans and septs or sections of clans, each occupying a well-defined tract of land. The tribe, however, is not so homogeneous, for it includes not only those who are descended from a common ancestor, but also the alien groups called *hamsayahs*. In their political organization the Baloch differ widely from the Pathans, for they are far less democratic and are ruled by hereditary tribal chiefs with real and not merely titular power, while the clans and septs are under headmen whose office is also hereditary. They too have a system of *jirgas* or councils of elders, both local and provincial, which is utilized for the

[1] See Sir Michael O'Dwyer, *India as I knew it* (1925), pp. 120–1.
[2] *Imperial Gazetteer of India*, vol. xix, pp. 166, 193.
[3] Loc. cit. C. A. Roe and H. A. B. Rattigan, *Tribal Law in the Punjab* (Lahore, 1895), pp. 16–17.

administration of British Baluchistan. The *jirgas* have judi-
cial functions and are consulted both on matters affecting the
individual tribe and on questions of common interest: a
representative body called the Shahi Jirga meets twice a year
to discuss matters affecting the whole province.

Land, as among the Pathans, is the joint property of the
tribe and is redistributed periodically in some parts, but not
in others, where it is in the permanent possession of tribal
sections among whom it has been parcelled out. Each clan is
required to raise an armed levy for purposes of offence and
defence proportionate to the share of land which it holds.
In areas which the strong arm of British authority does not
reach tribal and clan warfare goes on, and blood-feuds are rife;
the Baloch, like the Pathans, regard hospitality and the blood-
feud as almost sacred obligations. Outsiders are admitted as
members of the tribe in order to increase its fighting strength,
their adhesion being cemented by marriage with its women
and allotment of shares in the tribal land. Their habits are
more nomadic than those of the Pathans: the very name
Baloch means a nomad or wanderer. Throughout Baluchistan
small groups wander from place to place grazing their herds,
and it is common for the villagers to leave their houses in the
summer and camp out in tents erected near their fields.

Though they give their name to the country, the Baloch are
actually outnumbered by the Brahuis, another pastoral and
nomad race, who are banded together in a confederacy of
tribes. Each tribe is subject to a chief, who is assisted by a
council of elders, and all acknowledge the superior authority
of the Khan of Kalat. In other respects also they resemble the
Baloch, e.g. in their obsession by blood-feuds and in the practice of periodically redistributing the tribal land.

The population of the North-West Frontier Province consists mainly of tribes or tribal groups which are more or less
of the same stock as the trans-frontier tribesmen, but which

4078 I

have been converted from a predatory to an agricultural life. Each is united not only by common descent or the belief in it but also, to a large extent, by common interest in the village lands. The tribal system is utilized for the public welfare and plays an important part in the internal administration of the province. Local councils of elders are constituted for the adjudication of cases and for the promotion of education and medical relief as well as for protection from raids by the transfrontier Pathans. Train bands are maintained which defend the villages against attack and join in the hue and cry after the raiders. The Pathans observe their customary tribal law in matters of inheritance, &c., and follow the Pathan code of honour. Living under the reign of law they cannot prosecute blood-feuds, but they are prone to turbulence and the old Adam breaks out in other ways. It was reported in 1929-30 (when 490 murders were committed) that the employment of hired assassins was a prevalent practice and that in one district (Peshawar) the services of professional murderers could be obtained without difficulty for Rs. 400 (about £13) or less.[1] Hospitality is as much a national virtue as among their neighbours across the frontier. Every village has its guest-house, which is also a bachelors' hall, for young unmarried Pathans are not allowed to sleep at home but spend the night in the guest-house.

Individual ownership has replaced tribal ownership by an interesting process of segmentation. The tract held by a tribe was subdivided into lots, each held by a main subdivision of the tribe, such as a clan; the lots were subdivided into blocks, each held by a section; the blocks were split up into what are called 'sides', each held by a sub-section, which was generally a branch of a family; and finally the 'side' was subdivided into shares, each held by an individual proprietor.[2] The conception

[1] *India in 1929-30* (Calcutta, 1931), p. 390.
[2] *Imperial Gazetteer of India*, vol. xix, p. 192.

of individual property is even now of comparatively recent origin. The practice of periodically redistributing land used to be in force in some parts—two estates were so divided some thirty years ago—and tribal shares are still adhered to as a basis for the partition of land held in common and for the allotment of facilities for irrigation.

More than half of the population of the Punjab consists of agricultural tribes, such as Rajputs, Jats, and Gujars, who, whether Moslems, Hindus, or Sikhs, follow their traditional personal law rather than either Hindu or Islamic law. Groups of villages belong to a single tribe; west of the Sutlej the tribes occupy great blocks of country—one tribe is said to hold 1,000 square miles without a break; even to the east, where the tribe begins to merge in the village community, whole villages and groups of villages belong to them. There is a tribal right of pre-emption which has statutory recognition in the Punjab Alienation Act, a measure passed to prevent land passing from the tribal groups of agriculturists to money-lenders and others. It provides that no member of an agricultural tribe shall, except under certain carefully guarded conditions, alienate his land by sale or mortgage to any one who is not a member of the same group of agricultural tribes in the same district. As we proceed farther east towards the Gangetic valley the tribe is no longer a social unit but is replaced by the village community and its organization in the case of Hindus by that of caste.

The forest-clad hills and mountains of Assam are the home of many tribes whose original habitat is believed to have been the north-west of China, from which successive hordes made their way south down the valley of the Brahmaputra and other rivers. Their physical characteristics are Mongolian; short but sturdy, they have broad faces, high cheek-bones, flattish noses, and almond-shaped eyes. Scattered over an area of 25,000 miles, which is split up by mountain ranges and valleys, the different tribes live apart without unity or cohesion. There is no unifying force in either language or religion. They speak so many languages that their country is reminiscent of the Tower of Babel: the Naga tribes alone speak about twenty, as many as there are tribes. Their religion is mostly of the primitive kind known as Animism and has nothing in it to induce them to make common cause, as the trans-frontier Pathans do when stirred up by the preaching of fanatical *mullahs*.

Their history till recent times is one of almost constant warfare, due in some cases to internecine strife between tribes and clans, and in others to a northward movement which began two centuries ago, the tribes from the south pressing on those to the north of them. In this way the Lushais drove out and displaced the Kuki-Chins till the northward movement was stopped by British authority in Cachar. Besides this, the tribes were often on the warpath against their peaceful neighbours in the plains, swooping down in sudden raids and returning to their mountain strongholds with the heads of victims and bands of captives. They were formidable only because of the inaccessible nature of their country and the unwarlike character of the people of the plains. Their weapons were merely spears, swords, bows and arrows, with a certain number of muskets; their defensive works consisted of stockades, pitfalls, and calthrops made of bamboo, which were strewn on the paths leading to their villages: in an expedition against the Abors our men found their advance stopped by a stockade, made of tree trunks topped by bamboo spikes, which was over a mile long. The early history of our relations with them is a monotonous record of murderous raids and punitive expeditions. The later history is one of the extension of control over them, the gradual occupation of their country, and the introduction of peace, order, and civilization.

Among some tribes head-hunting was at one time almost as common as among the Dyaks. The practice appears to have been inspired by different motives. As pointed out by Dr. Hutton,[1] one underlying idea was that the soul resides in the head and that the taking of human heads is a means of acquiring souls, which adds to the soul-force of a village and promotes the welfare of its inhabitants and the fertility of its crops. Another was the desire to provide the dead with slaves in the next world; it was on this account that human heads were buried with the bodies of Kuki and Garo chiefs. Sometimes there appears to have been no religious significance in the practice, and heads were taken as a visible proof of military prowess or the attainment of manhood. The Lushais carried them off simply as trophies, and among the Nagas, the most persistent of all the head-hunting tribes, the taking of a head was considered an essential preliminary to marriage. It was a proof that a youth had reached manhood and was eligible for the married state and for full membership of the tribe; Naga girls had strong objections to marrying men who had not taken heads. Human sacrifices were also offered by the Nagas in the belief, common among primitive peoples, that they brought down rain and increased the productivity of the soil. They have learnt that substitutes are equally efficacious and are now content with an animal or even a dummy. The Angamis sacrifice a calf or a puppy, the Lhotas spear a wooden post, and in some Konyak villages, which were annexed as recently as 1909, the young men prove their fitness for marriage by spearing or cutting off the head of a wooden figure. Men, it has been said, who had been accustomed to decorate their houses with skulls feel almost content in using pumpkins for the purpose.[2] Beyond the frontier, where the British exercise no control, head-hunting and in some places

---

[1] J. H. Hutton, 'The Significance of Head-Hunting in Assam', *Journal of the Royal Anthropological Institute* (1928), pp. 399–408; J. P. Mills, *The Ao Nagas* (1926), pp. 225–6.

[2] Col. L. W. Shakespear, *History of the Assam Rifles* (1929), p. vii.

human sacrifice survive; the victims are not only captives taken in war, but also slaves or serfs and even unpopular members of the community.

Some of the tribes are migratory; as a Kuki once said to Professor Hodson, 'We are like the birds of the air; we make our nests here one year, and who knows where we shall build next year?'[1] Their nomadic life is associated with the practice of shifting cultivation called *jhum*, which is common throughout the hills of Assam. Clearings are made in the forest by felling and burning trees and undergrowth; the ashes are worked into the soil with a hoe, and seeds are dibbled in. As the soil is fertilized by the wood ash, bumper crops are raised for a time, but its productive capacity is soon exhausted. Crops can be raised on the same patch for only two or three years, after which a fresh clearing has to be made and the abandoned land relapses into jungle. When all the available land in the neighbourhood is exhausted, the village is shifted. The people seek more distant woods and make new clearings and new houses—an easy matter where bamboos are abundant—leaving their old houses to ruin and decay.

Others have permanent villages but still practise shifting cultivation, clearing and cultivating different parts of the forest in rotation, though some are so far advanced as to lay out the hill-sides in a series of terraced fields and to irrigate them by an ingenious system of water channels. The existence of permanent villages does not preclude migration, for when the population grows too large to be supported by the land in the vicinity, parties move off and found fresh colonies. The different villages have well-defined areas of forest in their exclusive possession, which serve both as their farm-land and as their hunting ground. Different families have holdings within the limits of each, and the rights of ownership are recognized to a surprising degree. What seems an uncared-for

[1] T. C. Hodson, *The Naga Tribes of Manipur* (1911), p. 2.

wilderness is really the jealously guarded property of a village or family, and no quarrels are more bitter or enduring than those about the forest land.[1]

The tribes have no centralized government, no unity of command or authority. There is so little tribal solidarity that the tie between the tribesmen is little more than belief in descent from a common ancestor, the use of a common language, and the rule of endogamy, marriage outside the tribe being forbidden. Each tribe is divided into a number of clans which consist of families connected by agnatic kinship and which observe the rule of exogamy, i.e. no man may marry a woman belonging to his clan. The Lushais furnish an exception to this general rule, for they allow different clans to intermarry. Their marriage law is, however, very lax, for a man can marry practically any woman he likes except his mother and sister, who alone come into the Lushai table of prohibited degrees; there is also a prejudice against the marriage of first cousins on the father's side, but this is due only to financial considerations, because, the marriage being within the family, nothing has to be paid for the bride, whereas the family receives a bride price for a woman who marries into another family.

The clan is therefore the unit for matrimonial purposes, but the unit for general social purposes is the village, which may consist of members of the same clan or of several different clans. The village polity is based on the institution of village chiefs or headmen, who act as the representatives of the people in their dealings both with the gods and with outsiders: to most of the tribes the idea of a village without a headman would be inconceivable. Sometimes they hold office by hereditary right, subject to the condition of competence, sometimes by popular election, which may take the simple form of acclamation. The extent of their authority is determined largely by their personality, and in any case it rests on the consent of the

[1] *Assam Administration Report for 1921-2* (Shillong, 1922), p. 64.

villagers themselves. They decide matters of common interest, allot land to different families when new land is cleared, &c. On the headman too devolves the duty of hospitality to strangers, and among the Lushais the support of widows, orphans, and others who are left destitute, so that his house is like a poorhouse. Those supported by him are in the position of retainers, whose services or labour he has a right to command. Formerly he used to give shelter to murderers flying from the avengers, thieves, vagabonds, and debtors, who were his serfs. Serfdom is still found in the country of the trans-frontier Nagas, where refugees and destitute persons place themselves under the protection of a headman or other influential person and swear allegiance to him in return for maintenance, land, or a wife.

Social status among some tribes, such as the Nagas and Lushais, is acquired by the performance of certain rites and ceremonies, by which a man is supposed in some mysterious way to communicate his own prosperity to the village at large. Only a man rich in crops and cattle can afford them, and it is believed that their performance will ensure similar richness for his fellow villagers. The completion of a series of five sacrificial feasts confers special prestige among the Lushais. A man who has given them may have posts erected in front of his house on which are impaled the skulls of the *mithun* (domesticated bison) sacrificed by him; it is the ambition of every Lushai to have a long row of these posts before his house. A man who gives some further feasts can have a window in the side of his house, a privilege otherwise confined to headmen.

The social and other activities of the Naga tribes are associated with an extraordinary variety of inhibitions and taboos and with the performance of rites and ceremonies designed to ward off misfortune and to promote their prosperity in general, and the fertility of their crops in particular. The word *genna*, which means a forbidden thing and is applied primarily to forbidden practices, is also used in an extended sense of holidays observed during the performance of ceremonies and sacrificial feasts. Every sacrifice is the occasion of a *genna*, during which the social group concerned, whether a village or a household, breaks off its relations with other social groups. Some *gennas* are permanent, e.g. certain articles of food are taboo; some are periodic, such as those connected with agriculture; others are occasional, for they take place only in the event of a crisis or special contingency, such as the apprehension or actual occurrence of an epidemic. Different *gennas* are observed by different tribes and villages, though some are general, and, taken all in all, they constitute an elaborate code of customary law. Non-observance of them, and breach of their rules are believed to cause calamity and are treated as social offences. They affect not only the activities of ordinary life and the relations of villagers both to one another and to outsiders, but also the relations of the sexes, for at certain times males and females are kept apart and marital intercourse is forbidden. During a village *genna* not only is work at a standstill, but no one may either enter or leave the village. *Gennas* are also in force which determine the work which may be done at different times of the year. The year is divided into two seasons, one in which agricultural operations may be undertaken, the other in which other pursuits are legitimate. During the agricultural season no one may work at a handicraft, no one may hunt or fish, thus giving game and fish a close season, no one may carry on a trade, and even dancing is tabooed.[1]

The Khasis call for special mention on account of their unique characteristics. They speak a peculiar language which has no affinity with the Tibeto-Burman tongues of the other

[1] For a detailed account of the *gennas* see T. C. Hodson, *The Naga Tribes of Manipur* (1911), pp. 164–86.

hill tribes. It is allied to the Munda languages of Chota Nagpur[1] and belongs to the Mon-Khmer group of languages, which have been traced into Malacca, Australonesia, and even Australia. They are far more advanced than the other tribes of Assam. Intelligent and industrious, they are keen traders (unlike the Assamese in general) and prosperous cultivators, growing rice on terraced fields on the hill-sides and exporting vast quantities of oranges from their orange groves. They are divided between twenty-five petty States, which have had some dignity conferred on them by treaties or agreements defining their relations with the Government of India. Their internal government is semi-democratic, for on the one hand they are under chiefs, but on the other the chiefs are elected and are bound to act on the advice of Councils called Darbars. Their social organization has been described as 'one of the most perfect examples still surviving of matriarchal institutions'.[2] They are as usual divided into exogamous clans, but these claim blood relationship by descent from a common ancestress and not a common ancestor. Priestesses officiate at sacrifices and the male officiants are only their deputies. The mother is the head of the family and in some parts is the only owner of property. Children belong to their mother's clan, and succession is matriarchal: a chief, for example, is succeeded by his sister's son. If a man has a separate household, his wife and daughters inherit his property. If he lives with his mother, he is regarded, whether he is married or single, as still belonging to the family of his mother, and his property passes to her or her sisters and their children. It has been suggested, with some reason, that this custom is due to the laxity of the marriage tie. Marriage may be dissolved at the will of either party, and divorces are effected on the flimsiest

[1] It is also noticeable that the Khasis erect monoliths as monuments to the dead like some Munda-speaking tribes.
[2] Lt.-Col. P. R. T. Gurdon, *The Khasis* (1914), Introduction, p. xx.

pretexts:[1] a case is known of a man having been married thirty-seven times before the age of 40. Wives change their husbands so much that there must often be doubt as to the paternity of children, and the embarrassment this would cause is avoided by succession in the female line.

Matriarchal succession is also in vogue among the Garos. On the death of a Garo woman her property passes to a daughter, but the widower can retain it if he marries a woman belonging to his deceased wife's family. On a man's death his property may pass through a daughter to a son-in-law, but in that case the son-in-law is obliged to marry his mother-in-law even though his wife is alive.

[1] There has been a mass movement towards Christianity owing to the labours of the Welsh Presbyterian Mission, and these remarks do not apply to Christian Khasis.

IV

TRIBES OF THE INTERIOR

THE region of hills and forests which stretches almost across
India from Bombay to Orissa is the home of many tribes
either of Dravidian or pre-Dravidian origin. They are the
descendants of early inhabitants, who took refuge in the hills
when wave after wave of Aryan conquest swept over the
plains, and there maintained their independence and preserved
their language, animistic religion, and tribal customs. Some
are extremely primitive and have scarcely any corporate life;
others are organized in village communities of a well-developed
type. Among many tribes there has been an infiltration of
Hinduism, which has acted as a solvent upon religious and
social customs and has tended to disintegrate tribal organization. Whole tribes or sections of tribes have been converted
into depressed castes as a result of Hinduization. The tribal
system has also been weakened by the opening up of the
country and contact with different cultures, while the British
system of law and administration has impaired the authority
of tribal law and institutions. Some tribes, however, have been
little affected by outside influences and still observe their
tribal law and customs, especially in matters of marriage,
inheritance, the tenure of land, and the adjudication of
disputes. Unlike the Hindus, they have no caste system;
they are free from scruples as to the food they may eat
and the company it may be eaten in; they have priests of
their own blood; they venerate neither Brahmans nor the
cow. So far from acknowledging any virtue in Brahmans,
many have a strong objection to them and will not even eat
food cooked by them: during the Orissa famine of 1865-7,
when the cooks at relief centres were Brahmans, Santals

starved in large numbers rather than eat the food which they prepared.

The tribes as a general rule are endogamous and are subdivided into exogamous clans or septs, i.e. a man may marry only a woman belonging to his tribe but of another clan or sept than his own. The latter rule is subject to some exceptions, e.g. the Santals and Oraons have no objection to a man marrying a woman of his mother's sept: according to a proverb of the former, 'No one troubles about a cow track or his mother's sept'. The septs are totemistic, i.e. they have as a totem some animate or inanimate object, such as an animal, bird, fish, reptile, tree, plant, or mineral, by whose name they are generally called, e.g. Mori means the peacock (*mor*) sept and has the peacock as a totem. The totem is a revered emblem and is not worshipped: injury to it, and sometimes even insult to it, renders a man liable to punishment. There are in consequence numerous taboos. A peacock-sept may not kill or eat a peacock, and among the Bhils a woman catching sight of one in the forest should veil her face or turn her head away. Again, a man of the shell-sept of the Santals may not eat shell-fish or even use shell ornaments. One Khond sept, which has a twig as its totem, will not use twigs for the construction of a wattle and dab house or even stay in the temporary huts made of the leafy branches of trees which are set up in the fields for watching the crops. Different septs of Oraons, according to their totem, will not touch iron with their lips or tongue, will not use oil extracted from a certain creeper, and will not eat pig's tripe. The Santals are singular in having passwords by which members of different septs can recognize one another; these passwords are the names of places, ancestors, chiefs, and other notable persons.

A certain laxity characterizes the relations of the sexes before marriage, but marriage imposes responsibility, and strict chastity and fidelity are required from married women. A desire to prevent irregular connexions between members of the same clan or even of the same family is probably the motive cause of the institution among many of the tribes of dormitories, sometimes described as bachelors' halls, in which the unmarried youths of a village sleep at night; similar dormitories are sometimes maintained for girls. Separate buildings are reserved for the purpose, or, as an alternative, the young people are accommodated in a building belonging to a respectable elderly couple who can keep an eye on them.

The tribes have no central system of government but have a form of local government based on the village with a headman. The headmanship is held for life and in practice is hereditary, subject to the rule that if the people are dissatisfied with a headman, they can elect another in his place, and that a son does not succeed his father if incompetent or unworthy. The headman himself has a patriarchal authority but is subject to the general will of the community, and important matters affecting the common weal are referred to and decided by a general assembly of tribesmen or a representative council.

Their religious beliefs people the hills and forests with numberless spirits, nearly all mischievous and malevolent. They believe firmly in witchcraft, and the witch-finder or exorcist is often called into action. Their religious festivals almost invariably end with bouts of heavy drinking: hunting and harvest festivals, in particular, are characterized by orgies of drunkenness. The immoderate use of intoxicants is also unfortunately part of the ordinary life. The aboriginals have no power of self-restraint: when they drink, they drink to excess.

Proceeding from west to east the first important tribe is that of the Bhils of Bombay, Rajputana, and Central India, who have a strength of nearly 2 millions. There is no doubt that they were once a ruling race, and a reminiscence of past sovereignty may be traced in the custom by which some Rajput

chiefs, when installed, used to be marked on the forehead
with some blood drawn from the toe or thumb of a Bhil: the
giving of the *tika*, as this symbol of chieftainship is called, was
a cherished privilege of certain Bhil families.[1] The Bhils fell
on evil times when they came into conflict with the Marathas,
who hunted them down and did their best to exterminate them
either in open battle or by secret treachery. A favourite trick
was to invite them to feasts and then put them to the sword.
In this way a Maratha Governor destroyed some 7,000 Bhils in
1804: those who were not killed outright but merely wounded
were dispatched by being thrown into wells and left to drown.
Another Governor two years later organized a *battue* for their
wholesale destruction and boasted that he put 15,000 to
death in 15 months. Those Bhils who took up arms were
treated with the utmost ruthlessness: if caught, they were tied
to red-hot guns, or chained to an iron seat, heated red-hot in
a fire, or they were flogged, mutilated by cutting off their ears
and noses, and flung down wells and precipices.

The Bhils, filled with an undying hatred of the Marathas,
became outlaws and marauders and retaliated with similar
atrocities. Sallying forth from the recesses of the hills, they
pillaged the lowland villages, killed their inhabitants, and lifted
their cattle. The people of the plains were terrorized, cultivation near the hills was abandoned, roads became impassable,
and security could only be had by paying blackmail. Their
reclamation in Khandesh was begun by Outram, who endeared
himself to the Bhils by the feasts which he gave them as well
as by his prowess as a tiger-slayer: a man who, when mauled
by a tiger, could say that he did not mind the scratches of a big
cat, was a man after their own hearts. He made the Bhils the

---

[1] Even the Maharana of Udaipur (or Mewar), the premier Hindu
prince and the acknowledged head of the Rajputs, underwent this ceremony, but it was abandoned six centuries ago. In Dungarpur the custom
lingered till comparatively recent times.

agents of their own civilization and with this object raised in 1825 a Bhil corps, of which the nucleus was nine men who had been his companions when shooting. This corps acted as a local militia, put down raids, and kept order among the Bhils; while tribal quarrels and blood feuds were amicably settled by councils on the basis of pecuniary compensation. Two other Bhil corps which were started later, the Malwa Corps in 1837 and the Mewar Corps in 1840, did similar work in other parts of the Bhil country, which was gradually pacified. The early history of these corps illustrates the simplicity and restlessness of the Bhils. Men of the Malwa Corps used calmly to go off home to reap their harvests leaving their wives to answer for them at musters; in the Mewar Corps the only uniform the Bhils would wear was a meagre loin cloth, their weapons were bows and arrows, and they deserted in a body unless they received their pay at the end of each day.

The Bhils are an interesting example of a tribe in a state of transition, for while some are still a wild forest tribe maintaining their traditional customs, others have become civilized and Hinduized. In Mewar and the southern Rajputana States three distinct classes are now recognized, viz. the village Bhils, the cultivating Bhils, and the wild or mountain Bhils. The first live in villages in the plains, of which they are generally the watchmen; the second are peaceful tillers of the soil; the third live in more or less independence, and follow a primitive tribal life varied by lapses into lawlessness and predatory habits. Simple justice between the Bhils of different territories is meted out by means of Border Courts, which settle tribal disputes and feuds and deal with such offences as cattle-lifting and the abduction of women.

The Bhils of Bombay are also being steadily civilized. Some sections have given up their ancestral life of hunting and nomadic cultivation and are being induced to take up settled agriculture. Large numbers have taken to labour, so much so

that in Khandesh they now form, with the Mahars, the labouring class in nearly all villages. Others subsist by collecting and
selling forest produce, such as wood, grass, &c., and the streets
of towns, which the Bhils formerly never entered except to
plunder, are now filled with crowds of them coming to market.
The subsequent account applies only to the more primitive
Bhils of the forest tracts.

The name Bhil means a 'bowman', and their belief is that
the use of the bow is the proper occupation of a man and that
a life of lawlessness and plunder is their hereditary lot. They
claim descent from a son of the god Mahadeo, who was distinguished by wildness and wickedness and was condemned, as
a punishment for having killed a cow, to be an exile and a thief
all the days of his life. The legend is obviously of Hindu
origin and has vicious implications, for a Bhil justifies robbery
by the plea, 'I am not to blame, I am the thief of Mahadeo'.
They have consequently a somewhat sinister reputation, as
may be seen from the well-known and perhaps mythical story
of the description given by a student in answering a university
examination paper, viz. 'The Bhil is a black man but more
hairy. He carries a bow, with which he shoots you in the back
when he meets you in the jungle and afterwards throws your
body into a ditch. By this you may know the Bhil.' Martial
traditions are still strong among them, and in the tract called
Mahi Kantha in Bombay they are said to be equally ready to
fight each other and their neighbours either to please a chief
or to shelter a criminal. They are also born hunters, trackers,
and woodsmen with astonishing powers of endurance. Traits
which make the Bhil attractive to the European are his pluck,
his candour, and his *naïveté*. He is singularly artless and truth-
ful, if he has not come into contact with the more sophisticated
Hindus of the plains, so much so that his denial of a charge
may almost be taken as a presumption of innocence: on the
other hand, if guilty, he will make full and frank confession.

Sir Evan Maconochie tells an amusing story of the child-like docility of the Bhil. Dr. Pollen, when on tour, had with him half a dozen Bhil prisoners who were under trial on a charge of dacoity (gang robbery) and were guarded by some men of the Bhil corps. One day, when he moved on to a new camp, both guard and their prisoners were missing; but they turned up later, the prisoners escorting the men of the guard, who had given way to the besetting sin of the Bhils and were lying dead drunk in two carts.[1]

They are subdivided into numerous exogamous clans, some of which claim a common descent, while others apparently have coalesced as a result of common action, either offensive or defensive, and common habitation. In some parts, like Mewar, the members of each clan live in separate villages, which are collections of homesteads each standing on a separate hillock with jungle near by to provide cover—an arrangement devised for purposes of defence, which, when the villages consist of hundreds of homesteads, results in their being spread over a huge area and being subdivided into different hamlets. Each clan and each village has its own headman, but disputes and quarrels are settled by the usual agency of *panchayats*, which are the ultimate tribal authority. Many, who practise the nomadic tillage already mentioned, shift their villages from place to place in the forests. They are especially prone to do so on account of superstitious fears or the occurrence of epidemics, while a sudden panic or alarm may send them out on the warpath. Their restlessness and excitability in the face of anything which is strange or unusual will be remembered by readers of Rudyard Kipling's *The Tomb of his Ancestors*.

The less civilized abhor manual labour, a trait which has proved a serious difficulty in times of famine. In the great famine of 1899–1900, when their little crops failed and also

[1] *Life in the Indian Civil Service* (1926), p. 75.

their supply of forest produce, such as roots, bulbs, and even grass, they sold all that they had rather than work as labourers on relief work. 'When everything was exhausted, the Bhil either took to the warpath and looted far and near, wherever opportunity afforded, or, if wanting in energy, wandered off into the forests probably to die.'[1] But the lesson they learnt was taken to heart, and thousands resorted to relief works in another famine two years later.

As among some of the trans-frontier Pathans, offences can be compounded by money payments, and there is a recognized scale of blood-money for murder. Unless and until this is paid, the victim's relatives have a vendetta against the murderer and the male members of his family. One of them is tracked down and killed with an arrow specially ornamented for the occasion, whereupon the avenger of blood raises a peculiar shrill cry to celebrate his triumph, like a Red Indian raising a war-whoop on killing an enemy. Private vengeance of this kind is of course a penal offence, and nowadays a blood feud is usually satisfied by carrying off the cattle of the murderer or of his family.

The women enjoy considerable independence. They have been known to take part in tribal fights armed with slings, but their more usual task is to tend the wounded and give them water. When engaged in this humane work they are inviolate and no arrow touches them. In some parts a woman may choose her own husband, and she can leave him for another if the latter repays her husband the expenses of her marriage. Girls sometimes elope with the young men they fancy, but the girl's father and brother retaliate by burning down the young man's hut and have to be appeased by monetary compensation. Some latitude is, however, allowed if a couple elope from a certain fair in Mahi Kantha. A river forms a kind of Gretna Green, for if the two can cross it without being caught, the

[1] Capt. E. Barnes, 'The Bhils of Western India', *Journal of the Society of Arts* (1907), p. 328.

parents agree to the marriage: otherwise the man is sum-
marily dealt with.

Women believed to be witches are treated with barbaric
savagery. The witch-finder is a recognized functionary of the
Bhils whose services come into requisition when illness or cattle
disease occur. The people are then assembled and the witch-
finder denounces a woman, who is frequently subjected to an
ordeal of varying forms. She may, for example, be tied up in
a sack and thrown into the water; if she sinks, she is held guilt-
less, if she manages to get her head above water or to swim,
she is adjudged a witch. The most ghastly form of ordeal is
what is called witch-swinging, which is fortunately very rare
nowadays and is punished with the rigours of the law. The
wretched woman is suspended head downwards from the
branch of a tree with her ankles tied and a pad of red pepper
over her face. A fire of green wood is lit beneath and she is
swung backwards and forwards until she confesses she is a witch
or dies, the witch-finder in the meanwhile torturing her with
sticks taken from the fire. Sometimes her agony is cut short
by a cut with a sword or by swinging her against a stone and
dashing out her brains.[1]

The Gonds are another great tribe, numbering three
millions, chiefly in the Central Provinces and the States of
Central India. Here they were once a ruling race, and alone
of the tribes in this part of India evolved within historic times
a centralized and civilized government. Four kingdoms were
established by Gond chiefs in the country which lies to the
north of the Central Provinces and is called Gondwana after
them. Walled towns, forts, and great irrigation works still
remain as witnesses of Gond power and civilization.

[1] Fuller accounts of the Bhils will be found in *Rajputana Gazetteers:
Mewar Residency* (Ajmer, 1908), vol. iiA; 'The Bhils of Western India' by
Capt. E. Barnes, *Journal of the Society of Arts* (1907); and *Tribes and
Castes of Bombay* by R. E. Enthoven.

'In the depths of a forest', writes Sir Bamfylde Fuller, who knew their country well, 'one is suddenly confronted with the high red sandstone walls of an abandoned city—an Indian uninhabited Carcassone. The walls extend for nearly six miles round. They are well-built and well-preserved, regularly crenellated, with arched gateways, over which is the Gond crest, the sculptured figure of an elephant treading down a tiger. Within them there is nothing but scrub jungle, through which sometimes, as in mockery, the tiger roves supreme.'[1]

The Gond kingdoms endured for three centuries till they were overthrown by the Marathas, who treated the Gonds as they did the Bhils, killing them by open attack and secret treachery.

Among the Gonds the process of transition from a forest tribe to an agricultural and labouring community of timid and inoffensive habits has gone even farther than among the Bhils. Half of them have given up Gondi, the tribal language; they have accepted many Hindu gods and customs, and they have to some extent adopted the caste system. The unreclaimed Gonds of the forest are held of little account by their Hindu neighbours: a local saying is 'In Chattisgarh the Gond is lord of the jungle. He has a fire under his bed and a leaf-pipe for his tobacco as he cannot afford either a blanket or a hookah. Kick him well at the start and he will do what you tell him.' The Hinduized Gonds are divided into two main sections, the Raj Gonds and the Dhur Gonds, names which are fully descriptive of status. Dhur Gond means dust Gond and is applied to the masses, who are chiefly small cultivators and labourers. Raj Gond means the royal Gond and is applied to the aristocracy, who are chiefly landholders. The latter are now a recognized caste and ultra-zealous in their observance of Hindu customs. 'With scrupulous exactitude they perform the prescribed ablutions of their adopted faith and carry their passion for purification so far as to have their faggots duly

[1] Sir Bamfylde Fuller, *Some Personal Reminiscences* (1930), p. 36.

sprinkled with water before they are used for cooking.'[1]
Among the lower classes there are castes formed of the
descendants of Gonds who used to hold special tribal offices.
One consists of the Pardhans, whose ancestral function is that
of bards, for they recite genealogies, stories of the gods, and
the deeds of ancestors, besides assisting at religious festivals;
another is the Ojha, a name for the wizard or exorcist; a third
is the Naik or soldier.

The tribal organization is now chiefly seen in the social
divisions within or outside which marriages take place. They
are of an unusually complex character, for they are based on
religion as well as totemism. There are four main groups, each
of which worships a different number of gods and has a different totem. The totems are a tortoise for the worshippers of
four gods, a crane for the worshippers of five, a tiger for the
worshippers of six, and a porcupine for the worshippers of
seven. There is no intermarriage of members of the same
group, i.e. a member of one group must marry into another
group with a different number of gods. This rule is subject to
a further condition imposed by a system of totemistic septs.
Each group is subdivided into septs, which also have totems,
and there is a similar rule of exogamy based on the totem;
according to this, a member of one sept may not marry into
a sept in another group if it has the same totem, even though
it worships a different number of gods. The Gonds of Balaghat
practise polygamy, the idea being that a plurality of wives is
proof positive of wealth and position. A man is sometimes the
proud husband of as many as six wives and goes to market
with all of them walking in line behind him to show his
importance.

In no part of the interior of India have the tribes preserved
their ancestral customs and language to such an extent as in

[1] S. Hyslop, *Papers relating to the Aboriginal Tribes of the Central
Provinces* (1866), p. 5.

Chota Nagpur and the adjoining district of the Santal Parganas. This area proved a sanctuary in which they lived almost in isolation until modern times. The largest group of tribes consists of the Santals, Mundas, and Hos, numbering over 3 millions, who call themselves by the same name, Ho, Hor, or Horo, meaning simply 'man': Santal and Munda are names given to them by aliens. They speak cognate tongues known generically as Munda languages, and they have maintained a singularly complete form of social organization, based on the village and federal union of villages.

Its origin may be sought in the foundation of a village in the forest by a family or group of families connected by descent from a common ancestor in the male line. This body of settlers cleared away the forest, brought the land under cultivation, and held it as joint proprietors. The head of the family or group of families became the headman of the village community, but the ultimate authority rested in the village council composed of elders of families, which administered customary law, decided disputes in accordance with it, and maintained social order and discipline. As the original family or families increased in number, parties of them moved off, made fresh clearings in the forest, and formed new villages which became independent communities with their own headmen and councils. Composed, as they were, of blood relations, the parent village and the neighbouring daughter villages naturally formed a federal union, which acted as one body in matters of common concern. In the union the organization of the villages was reproduced, i.e. there was a chief headman and a council, which acted as a court of appeal for villages within the union. There the capacity for combination seems to have stopped. The tribesmen did not join in any combination larger than that of a federal union of members of the same sept and had no centralized government.

This type of social government may perhaps be seen in its

most complete form among the Santals in the district of the Santal Parganas. The unit is the village under a *manjhi* or headman, whose presence is necessary at all public functions, such as festivals, sacrifices, &c. Should the village be under a headman of another race for purposes connected with the collection of rent and civil administration, a Santal headman is elected for the discharge of religious and social functions: his title is eloquent of the part liquor plays in religious life, for he is called 'the liquor headman'.

With the headman is associated a small body of village functionaries. The first is the *jog manjhi*, which may be translated as *custos morum*, for it means 'the manners headman'. He presides at ceremonies of birth and marriage, but his special duty is to look after the morals of unmarried youths and maidens and bring delinquents to justice. For instance, if an unmarried girl expects a baby, he has to find out who is the father, and if the man belongs to another sept, bring him up to the village council for punishment. He is kept up to the mark by the villagers, for, should he neglect his duty, they tie him up to a post in the headman's cowshed, abuse him, and perhaps fine him. The second functionary is the priest, who offers sacrifices in the sacred grove. This is found on the outskirts of every village: it must include five trees of the primeval forest which was in existence when the village was founded; a cluster of trees is always left round these five. The third is a kind of beadle, who acts as a messenger for the headman, calls the villagers together on his instructions, &c. In addition to these, the headman, *jog manjhi*, and priest have each an assistant, who officiates for his principal if necessary.

The headman's powers are derived from the villagers, and he calls them together to discuss and decide on major questions of common interest as well as to try any one accused of a serious social offence. The village council consists of all the adult males, but is called 'the five men', a name which is an exact parallel to the Indian term *panchayat*. It meets at the village council-house, a simple kind of shed in which is a stone or roughly carved piece of wood representing the spirits of the first headman or founder of the village and of his successors. Although the offices of the headman and his colleagues are in practice hereditary, the villagers have a meeting once a year, at which, after the performances of certain sacrifices, the headman resigns his post to the people and his fellow officers follow suit. Their offices are formally given back by the people and resumed by them a few days later. The villagers, on the other hand, surrender their lands to the headman, using a form of words which means that they retain only their bodies and their wives. The lands are formally accepted by him and formally given back.

In addition to his social duties the headman in the Santal Parganas has certain administrative duties, which give him a quasi-official position. He collects rents and taxes, reports village crime, and allots abandoned holdings. He deals direct with the civil authorities and can only be dismissed by the head of the district, who also appoints him. He is liable to dismissal for misconduct, such as embezzlement or oppression of his fellow villagers. If a headman dies, his heir normally succeeds him if competent; if another man is selected, the appointment is practically a confirmation of the villagers' choice.

The social organization does not end with the village. Villages are grouped in unions with headmen and councils consisting of village headmen and other persons of influence in the neighbourhood. These superior councils decide matters too important to be disposed of by a village council and also adjudicate on appeals from its orders. There is, further, a tribal gathering once a year on the occasion of common hunts. These hunts are convened by a man who is both master of the hunt and sacrificial priest. Hundreds of Santals gather together armed with spears, clubs, bows, and arrows and make a drive through the forest for days together, killing every bird and beast that they meet. After the hunt is over the assembled tribesmen decide any matter brought before them and excommunicate grave offenders. On this occasion any one can prefer a complaint or make a charge against either a village or a union headman, and the assembled Santals proceed straight away to hear and decide upon it.

Among the Mundas of Chota Nagpur the system of land tenures is based very largely on descent in the male line from the original founders of villages, and those who are so descended have special rights, which are protected by legislation. There are two privileged classes called *khuntkattidars* and *bhuinhars*. The former, who are in a minority, are descendants of those who cleared the forest and founded villages before landlords appeared on the scene: the name means 'clearer of the jungle'. They still retain full proprietary rights in the whole area included within the village boundaries, subject to the payment of a fixed quit-rent to superior landlords, and have tenants under them. The latter are often their relatives on the female side and are in no sense co-owners of the village. The *bhuinhars*, on the other hand, include not only the descendants of the original settlers and co-proprietors, but also the descendants of those who reclaimed land and formed villages in areas where landlords had already acquired proprietary rights. Consequently they have no proprietary rights but hold land either rent-free or on payment of a small quit-rent which cannot be enhanced.

The title-deeds of both alike, according to a local saying, are their grave-stones. This refers to the Munda custom of a common burial ground. The members of a sept are united in life by the performance of common sacrifices and in death by burial in a common cemetery attached to each village. The tombs are marked by grave-stones consisting of stone slabs, which either lie flat on the ground or are raised a little above it by stones at each corner. If a man dies away from the village, his bones are brought to it on the occasion of an annual festival and buried with those of his family and ancestors. As the right to burial is confined to members of the same sept and implies descent from the founders of the village, a Munda can only establish a claim to membership of a particular sept or village by proving that he has such a right.

Other village institutions are the sacred grove, the dancing ground, and the dormitories of young bachelors and maidens. The sacred grove, as among the Santals, consists of trees which were left standing when the forest was first cleared, and is the only temple of the people. The dancing ground is an open space where the villagers dance at times of festival and on moonlight nights. It is also the meeting-place of the village council. The bachelors sleep at night in the house of a villager who has a spare hut large enough for the purpose, the girls in a house belonging to some old childless couple or an elderly widow who keeps an eye on them and prevents scandals.

'These dormitories', says Rai Bahadur Sarat Chandra Ray, 'are in their own humble way seminaries for moral and intellectual training. After young bachelors and young maidens are assembled in their respective *giti-oras* [dormitories], after their evening meals, riddles are propounded and solved, folk-tales, traditions and fables are narrated and memorized, and songs sung and learnt, until bedtime.'[1]

The Munda village has a religious headman called the *pahan*, who performs sacrifices, and a secular headman called the *munda*: the name of the latter, who represents the people in dealings with Hindu and other outsiders, was applied by the latter to the whole tribe. Originally the head of the family which founded the village combined both offices, and they were separated either because on the death of one of them his

[1] 'Ethnography of the Mundas', *Modern Review* (Calcutta, 1911), p. 171.

eldest son declined to hold both offices, or because the people thought it undesirable that he should do so. If he decided to be the *munda*, the second son became the *pahan*, and both on their death were succeeded by their sons, the offices being hereditary. In some Munda villages they are still combined, and if the family of a *pahan* dies out, the secular headman sometimes resumes the priestly functions.

In both the *khuntkatti* and *bhuinhari* areas the Mundas have preserved the organization of village unions (*parhas*), which include eight to twelve villages. The unions have councils which decide all important questions of social life such as disputes about inheritance and boundaries, the right to burial in the village cemetery, breaches of social rules and marriage laws, and also sometimes cases in which witch-finders charge women with being witches. Their constitution differs in the two social areas. In the *bhuinhari* area the members of the union are Mundas of the same sept, and there is a permanent council composed of permanent office-bearers, whose titles are not Munda but Hindu owing to the influence of Hindu landlords. The names are borrowed, but the spirit which animates them is tribal. The council has a headman as permanent president, who is called the Raja and who receives complaints through the village headman or priest and convenes the council. All members of the sept have a right to be present at its meetings. The case having been heard, the president pronounces judgement. If found guilty, the accused may be excommunicated or fined or, as a mild punishment, required to drink the blood of a he-goat or cock, which must be white in colour. If he fails to pay a fine, he is soundly thrashed and excommunicated. Besides acting as a tribunal, the council discusses and settles questions of social and agrarian policy varying from that of abolishing dances as productive of immorality to that of united opposition to landlords.

In the *khuntkatti* area the union is not necessarily composed of members of the same sept, and the council is composed not of permanent office-bearers (except the president, who is the headman of the union) but of one or two headmen from each of the villages within its ambit. Minor private disputes in both areas are referred to courts of arbitration, the members of which are selected from among men summoned by either party.

The Hos of Singhbhum have a cognate system of village and union headmen and councils, which has been recognized by Government and forms part of the administrative machinery. The Ho villages are Government property, and the headman collects the rent, performs certain police duties, and looks after village roads and forests. The union headman supervises the village headmen and has corresponding duties for the area under him. The authority of the union councils is also recognized as regards civil cases of a minor character, especially those in which tribal customs are concerned. Rules, which were first made in 1837 and are still in force, provide for suits being referred to these councils and declare that decrees passed in conformity with their awards are not subject to appeal unless the awards are proved to be due to bribery or are contrary to common law or statutory rules. The Hos themselves, however, seem to be losing confidence in their headmen and prefer to take their cases to court. Another feature which seems to be due to Hindu influence is the introduction of caste divisions in their internal structure, for each of their many exogamous septs is now divided into two sections, one of which is socially superior to the other and will neither eat nor intermarry with the lower.

The limitations of space preclude a reference to the social structure and customs of the many other tribes of this part of India, but mention cannot be omitted of the Khonds (or Kandhs) of Orissa. They were notorious ninety years ago for human sacrifice and female infanticide. Human beings were sacrificed to the earth-goddess, the essential part of the rite being that pieces of their flesh should be cut off and buried in the fields to ensure their fertility. The ceremony of immolation was always revolting to an extreme degree. Sometimes the victims were first drowned in the blood of pigs; sometimes they were cut to pieces while still alive. The practice was suppressed, and the Khonds having been induced to sacrifice buffaloes instead of human beings, soon found that the burial of their flesh in the fields was just as effectual. Belief in the old rite still lingers however; in 1907 the Khonds of Ganjam petitioned the District Officer to allow the resumption of human sacrifice as an emergency measure on account of drought and scarcity.

Female infanticide was due not, as used to be the case among the Rajputs of North India, to the difficulties and expense of getting daughters married, but to the trouble and expense which they caused after they were married. According to the usual custom among Indian tribes, when a marriage takes place, a bride price is fixed for the bride, i.e. the bridegroom gives a consideration in money and cattle. The Khond who desired a wife raised the necessary amount from kinsmen of his sept; his father-in-law distributed it among the heads of families in his sept. The Khond women were at liberty to dissolve their marriages at will and contract fresh marriages; if one entered the house of an unmarried man, and established herself there, he was in honour bound to marry her. When a woman left her husband, he was entitled to a refund of the bride price from her father, and the latter was entitled to recover it from her new husband. The trouble did not end there, for every man's sept was answerable for his debts and bound to enforce his claims. The result may be seen from the remarks of Major Macpherson, who was largely responsible for the suppression both of female infanticide and human sacrifice, and whose name is consequently one of honour among the Khonds.

'These restrictions and exactions, whether to be made between persons belonging to different tribes or to different branches of the same tribe, must be even in the simplest cases productive of infinite difficulty and vexation; while they have given rise to three-fourths of the sanguinary quarrels and hereditary feuds which distract the Khond family. Hence say the Khonds: "To any man but a rich and powerful chief who desires to form connexions and is able to make large and sudden restitutions, and to his tribe, a married daughter is a curse. By the death of our female infants before they see the light, the lives of men without number are saved and we live in comparative peace."'

So effectually did the Khonds act on this principle that there were many populous villages where not a single female child could be seen.

It might be thought that a race given to such inhuman practices were without social virtues. The reverse was the case. According to their code there are nine cardinal sins, viz. (1) to refuse hospitality, (2) to break an oath or even a promise, (3) to lie except to save the life of a guest, (4) to break a pledge of friendship, (5) to break an old law or custom, (6) to commit incest, (7) to contract debts (because of the communal responsibility for them and the harm they do to the sept), (8) to shirk one's duty in time of war, and (9) to divulge a tribal secret. Their history, moreover, since they were brought under British rule, has in the territory called the Khondmals been one of considerable progress. In less than thirty years after annexation they voluntarily imposed a tax on liquor shops and devoted the proceeds to the promotion of primary education, and they levied another tax for roads to bring them into communication with the outside world. As recently as 1908 they started a prohibition movement, taking vows to abstain entirely from intoxicants because of the evils of drunkenness. Their spirit was willing but flesh was weak, and drunkenness still went on. They then petitioned Government to close every liquor shop in their country, and this was done. Nothing else, they declared, would save them from drunkenness, which had proved a curse, for it led to poverty, wife-beating, and the loss of their ancestral lands.

In some parts the Khonds have adopted the customs and language of their Hindu neighbours and have formed themselves into a caste. In more remote areas the Khonds maintain their traditional manner of life. They are, like other tribes, divided into numerous exogamous septs with different totems, and their government is patriarchal with villages under village headmen and unions under union headmen: the former are called fathers, the latter old fathers. They claim an indefeasible right in the soil and will not allow outsiders to take up holdings in their villages. The acquisition by a non-Khond of landed rights would, they hold, be equal to an acknowledgement of his blood relationship. They will, however, admit outsiders to the village in a subordinate capacity. By old custom a man may become a dependant or retainer of the headman, whom he has to help if required and who, for his part, is expected to find him a wife; this relationship goes on among the succeeding generations and is cheerfully accepted by them.

The Khonds hold that war and the chase are the proper occupations of a man, though they are debarred from fighting by Government, and to some extent from hunting by the increasing scarcity of game. They regard themselves as above such banausic pursuits as trade and industry, and will not admit to fellowship even the descendants of Khonds who work as potters, blacksmiths, and cowherds. There is attached to every large village a small colony of artisans, potters, weavers, oilmen, and labourers, but they are there merely to serve the needs of the Khonds, who treat them as inferiors, while sweepers and Pans (a servile class, who used to be their serfs) are considered unclean, and have consequently to live in a settlement away from the village site, and are not allowed to draw water at the village well.

There are numerous other tribes and fragments of tribes which have not attained anything like the same degree of civilization as those already mentioned. Some are in as elementary a stage of progress as the aborigines of Australia. In South India the Tamil Kallans and Maravans still use throwing-sticks, rather like boomerangs, to knock down small game such as hares. The Kadirs and Mala Veddans, also of South India, have their incisor teeth chipped to a point—a practice also found in the Malay Peninsula. The Yanadis and the Kanikars of Travancore make fire by friction, obtained by rubbing sticks of wood or bamboo, while the former eat the flesh of the game which they kill almost raw, merely heating or scorching it before a fire. The Kadavas or Bodavas in the forests of Coorg are so little used to clothes that the women's dress is only a few leaves, which they change four times a day, and the Paliyans in the Palni Hills of Madura are described as a miserable jungle folk who have no settled habitations, dwell in crevices in rocks or the rudest of huts, and live upon leaves, roots, vermin, and honey.[1] Many of these rude tribes, however, are being affected by modern influences and losing their primitive simplicity. As Mr. Thurston has pointed out,

'tribes which only a few years ago were living in a wild state, clad in a cool and simple garment of forest leaves, buried away in the depths of the jungle, and living, like pigs and bears, on roots, honey, and other produce, have now come under the domesticating and sometimes detrimental influence of contact with Europeans with a resulting modification of their conditions of life, morality, and even language.'[2]

There are other tribes equally primitive in North India. Such is the Korwa, whom Mr. Crooke has described as a mere

---

[1] *Imperial Gazetteer of India*, vol. xix, pp. 309, 372.
[2] *Castes and Tribes of Southern India* (1909), p. xv.

savage, a troglodyte who lives apart from his kinsfolk, who has not even prohibited degrees of marriages.[1] Another tribe which is pitiably undeveloped is that of the Juangs of the Orissa States, who are also called Patuas, i.e. leaf-wearers, because they cover their nakedness with leaves. The women of one section of the tribe were first introduced to clothes in 1871, when an English officer presented each of them with a strip of cotton cloth. After donning the new clothes, they passed before him in single file to the number of 1,900, made obeisance, and then solemnly burnt the bunches of leaves which they had discarded. Little more has been known about these people till the publication in 1931 of *The People of the Leaves* by Mr. V. Meik, who spent some time with a section of the Juangs in the State of Rairakhol. From his account they would appear to be in the lowest stage of human existence, scarcely a tribe but rather a pack living together for mutual defence and the common acquisition of food. He found that bunches of leaves, plucked fresh every day, were the only dress. Every morning the people lolled or strolled about naked, till fresh leaves were gathered and made up like sporrans or girdles, hanging down in front and behind and leaving the thighs bare. They lived in primeval forest, and their food consisted of roots, berries, birds' eggs, and the birds or small animals which they shot with their arrows. They only occasionally ate meat for a change, and they distilled spirit from the fruit of the *mahua* tree. They dug roots out of the earth with their hands and pieces of flint, and ate them raw: fires were not used for cooking. They had no cattle and cultivated no crops. Their weapons were knives, and bows and arrows. The knives were merely pieces of sharpened flint; the arrows were barbed with flint; the bows were made not from wood, but from a root which has some resiliency, and their strings were either thin roots or plaited grass or (rarely) uncured thongs of

[1] W. Crooke, *North-Western Provinces of India* (1897), pp. 218-19.

leather. Physically they were a feeble folk, the women fragile, the men small and weedy with poor muscular development and without sufficient physical strength to kill beasts of prey. They were terrified of almost every animal that roams the jungle and would plunge into the tangled undergrowth to escape them. There were a number of small separate communities, each under its own headman, living in forest clearings and protected from the attacks of wild beasts by fences of plaited creepers. As for their social customs, they had no marriage or rules of marriage. Intercourse was promiscuous, extending even to incest between fathers and daughters and between brothers and sisters, with no sense of shame. *209320*

V

THE VILLAGE COMMUNITY

INDIA has been called a land of villages, and if proof is needed of the truth of the description, it is found in the census figures which show that the rural population numbers over 300 million or nine-tenths of the total population. Practically the whole country is parcelled out among villages, about half a million in number. A more vivid impression of the predominance of village life is obtained from a railway journey through India. For hundreds of miles at a stretch village succeeds village, towns are few and far between, and many of the small towns are more like overgrown villages, in the midst of which the cattle are driven afield and from which the peasant goes out with his simple plough on his shoulder to till the neighbouring lands. Another thing which strikes the traveller is that throughout the greater part of the country there are miles and miles of cultivated land for every residential village that he sees. Except in Bengal, Assam, and some parts of Madras there are few separate homesteads or farms scattered over the country-side. The people are gregarious and live in houses closely packed together on a central site, occasionally with one or two hamlets close by, surrounded on all sides by fields. Here the peasant has his home and keeps his cattle; from it he sets forth in the morning to his labour on the land; to it he returns and drives his cattle back in the evening. The term village is not used in the sense which commonly attaches to it in England, but corresponds to the parish. It means not merely the inhabited site with its cluster of houses and buildings, but comprises the whole area within the village boundaries, including not only the residential village, but also the cultivated fields which form the peasants' holdings, the land under pasturage, and the land that lies waste.

The village is the unit of communal life in India. Each village forms a separate community, a self-centred and largely self-supporting society, of which the members are linked not merely by the habitual associations of a common life, but by an organization designed for the execution of common purposes. It is known to be of great antiquity and has persisted through the ages with little change until comparatively recent times. Its vitality and power of endurance through political and economic vicissitudes have often been commented upon. It is, according to Sir Henry Maine,

'the least destructible institution of a society which never willingly surrenders any one of its usages to innovation. Conquests and revolutions seem to have swept over it without disturbing or displacing it, and the most beneficent systems of government in India have always been those which have recognized it as the basis of Indian administration.'[1]

Lord Lawrence again wrote of the village communities:

'They are admirably adapted to resist the evil effects of bad seasons, epidemics, and other evils incidental to this country. Bound together by the ties of blood connexion, and, above all, common interest, like the bundle of sticks . . . they are difficult to break. Drought may wither their crops, famine and disease may depopulate their houses, their fields may be deserted for a time, but when the storm blows over, if any survive, they are certain to return.'[2]

'Among all castes their love for the soil, and veneration for everything connected with the village, is remarkable. These local attachments seem, indeed, to me to supply the place of love of country. It may be said that a native of India does not feel that he has a country. He cares nought for what is passing in the world or who is his ruler. His love, his hatred, his fears, his hopes, are confined to the village circle. He knows little and cares less

---

[1] *Ancient Law* (1891), p. 261.
[2] Loc. cit. Sir C. Aitchison, *Lord Lawrence* (1897), p. 27.

for what goes on beyond it. So many different dynasties have governed his country; it has so often been transferred from one ruler to another that so long as no one interferes with village matters, he is indifferent. On the other hand, let any attack be made upon the village, let a claim be preferred to a single acre of the most barren and unproductive of its lands, and every one is up in arms, ready to risk his life or spend his fortune in preserving those possessions inviolate.'[1]

The origin and constitution of the village communities have been the subject of special study. They were first dealt with by Sir Henry Maine in *Village-Communities in the East and West* (1871). This work, however, was concerned mainly with the type of village community found in the Gangetic plain which is now the United Provinces and only incidentally with the villages in other parts of the country, such as Central and South India, which have a different constitution. The whole subject was next treated exhaustively by Mr. B. H. Baden-Powell in *The Indian Village Community*, published in 1896, which was followed three years later by a shorter and more popular work, *The Origin and Growth of Village Communities in India*.

There are two main types of village, viz. the joint village found in the north-west of India, i.e. in the North-West Frontier Province, the Punjab, and the United Provinces, and the 'severalty' or *ryotwari* village found elsewhere. The joint village is not a village of a communistic type, i.e. a village in which the land is held in common without any one having individual rights, and in which the proceeds of cultivation are enjoyed in common. It is called joint because the village lands constitute the joint property of an organized proprietary body, often styled the 'brotherhood', an expression which indicates that this body originally constituted an aggregate of individuals related, or supposed to be related, to each other by descent

[1] R. Bosworth Smith, *Life of Lord Lawrence* (1885), vol. i, p. 100.

from a common ancestor. At a later stage, when portions of the village lands have passed by transfer to persons or groups of persons belonging to other families, the term 'brotherhood' acquires a more extended meaning and comes to signify an association based, not upon kinship, but upon the possession of common interests in the same definite area of land.

The members of this proprietary body are ordinarily grouped in divisions and subdivisions, each in possession of separated shares of the cultivable area, corresponding more or less with the shares determined by the rules of inheritance and partition under the joint family system, by the operation of which the shares are owned, not separately by individuals, but jointly by families. While the cultivable area is so divided, the inhabited site and the waste and pasture lands remain undivided and constitute the joint property of the proprietary body as a whole. This entire body is more than an association of coparceners. It is also, so to speak, a corporation organized for the management of the affairs of the village including the payment of the land revenue. The usual practice is for the business of the village to be transacted through a representative council (*panchayat*), though not infrequently the duty of collecting and paying the land revenue lies with a single chosen agent, a headman whose office has been created by Government and tends, like other offices, to become hereditary.

Villages of this type are called *pattidari*[1] in the United Provinces, where they prevail. There is also another class of joint village, which is not very numerous, to which the term *zamindari* is applied. This is one in which all the village lands are held and managed in common and not divided. The tenants, if any, are the tenants of the whole body of proprietors, their rents and other receipts are paid into a common fund, from which common expenses are met, and the annual profits

---

[1] From *patti*, meaning a piece or subdivision, a term used of a share in a joint village or estate; a *pattidar* is one who has such a share.

are divided among the co-sharers according to their respective shares.

The joint villages as now existing appear to have originated in one or other of several different ways. In one case the ancestors of the present proprietors acquired the land by conquest, the former occupants often becoming tenants under them; it is well known that under the pressure of the Muhammadan invasion bodies of Rajputs moved eastward into the Gangetic valley, where they conquered the tribes which had hitherto been in occupation of a large part of the country and reduced them to the position of villeins. In other cases the founders of the villages were colonists, either blood relations or associated groups of settlers, who cleared the land and brought it under cultivation. In a third class of cases the ancestor of the co-proprietors was either a man who received a grant of land from the ruling power, such as a Brahman for religious services or a Rajput for military services, or one who acquired land by purchase, or an official who was responsible only for the collection and payment of land revenue for a village and who converted his position to that of proprietor.

Where the village has remained entirely in the hands of descendants of the founders, whether conquerors, settlers, grantees, &c., the present proprietors are kith and kin bound together by the tie of common ancestry as well as of common ownership. But in many cases the proprietary body is of a composite character owing to the acquisition of shares in the village by strangers. Where this is the case the bond of union is only one of common interest, for though some of the co-sharers may be connected by blood relationship, others are not. The co-sharers, it should be added, have a right of pre-emption and are entitled to veto the admission of a newcomer, but their power of refusing consent has been weakened by the action of the law courts and in particular by the execution of decrees.

A special feature of the joint village is that of joint responsibility for the land revenue, in theory at least. When the first 'settlement'[1] of what is now the United Provinces was made nearly a century ago, it was decided that responsibility for the payment of the land revenue should rest not with individual coparceners but with the whole coparcenary body. The village was accordingly assessed to a lump sum, for which the co-parceners were jointly responsible. It was for them to decide what quota each coparcenary family should pay, and if any was in default with its quota, the others had to make it good. The whole estate is still theoretically responsible for the default of any co-sharer, but actually communal responsibility is rarely enforced and action is taken against the individual defaulter. The system of joint responsibility was extended to the Punjab when it was annexed. There too the co-proprietors are technically liable for the joint payment of land revenue, but 'the tendency is towards individualism, and with lighter and more elastic assessments the enforcement of collective responsibility has become practically obsolete. In practice the owner or owners of each holding are assessed separately to revenue and are responsible to Government for the revenue so assessed'.[2]

Two other characteristic features of the joint village are the village fund and the *panchayat*. The common fund is maintained from rentals and miscellaneous receipts from fisheries, trees, grazing, and market dues. From it common village expenses are met. These are very mixed in character: they may include the cost of charity, e.g. to Brahmans and beggars, of entertaining guests and strangers, of common entertainments, including popular amusements, and frequently also of bribing petty officials. The administration of this fund rests

---

[1] Arrangements for the assessment and collection of the land revenue and the registration of landed tenures.

[2] *Imperial Gazetteer of India*, vol. xx, p. 343.

with a council of elders, belonging to the proprietary families, called, as usual, a *panchayat*, which controls village administration though to a much diminished extent. It is an active institution among village communities of a tribal type, but in others it has lost much of its old power owing to the intrusion of other agencies and the growing tendency to refer disputes to the law courts instead of settling them locally. Not infrequently it is only convened occasionally to settle disputes and to decide about the expenditure of the village fund and the quota of land revenue to be paid by individual holdings.

There are, it is true, headmen who represent the villagers in their dealings with Government, but these are a modern creation for the purpose of revenue administration and not part of the original village constitution. The headman has a quasi-official position and his name bespeaks his recent origin: it is *lambardar* from *lambar*, the Indian pronunciation of the English word number, and it means the man who bears a number. The reason is that a man was appointed by Government for each village, whose duty it was, and still is, to pay the land revenue assessed on the village and to collect the due share of it from each proprietary family, and that he was given a number in the Government registers.

Owing to the existence of *panchayats* and the absence of village headmen other than the semi-official headmen, the joint village is sometimes described as democratic; but actually its constitution appears to be more like that of an oligarchy, for it does not include tenants, artisans, shopkeepers, and others who are not members of the proprietary body. They belong to the village, but being outside the 'brotherhood' are subordinate to the co-proprietors, who even decide whether they may have houses on the residential site. There are, in fact, two classes of men in the village, one with proprietary rights, the other without them, and control rests with the former exclusively.

'The idea of a proud Rajput kindred or group of, say, 80 or 100 co-sharing members, with 15 or 20 elders or heads of houses, regarding their cultivating tenants and the village watchmen, not to mention the washerman and the sweeper, as constituting part of the "brotherhood" is something quite grotesque. . . . The "brotherhood" consists of just as many families as have actual shares in the land—as are existing co-proprietors and no more.'[1]

According to Sir Henry Maine, the village community has the double aspect of a group of families united by the assumption of a common kinship and of a company of persons exercising joint ownership over land. It is not necessarily an assemblage of blood relations, but it is either such an assemblage or a body of co-proprietors formed on the model of an association of kinsmen.[2] This description applies only to the joint village in the north of India. The prevalent form of village in the greater part of India is another type in which there are no co-proprietors, the village which Mr. Baden-Powell has named the severalty or *ryotwari* village. The unit for land revenue purposes is not the village, but the holding of each ryot or cultivator, which is separately assessed to, and separately responsible for, land revenue. There is no joint liability for land revenue; there is no waste land held in commonalty which can be divided if required for cultivation, though there may be common rights of use in the waste, e.g. for grazing.

Each village, moreover, is under a headman, who holds office by hereditary right and is the acknowledged head of the community. He is an important link in the chain of administration, for he represents Government to the people and the people to Government; he collects the land revenue of his village and he controls the village watchmen. Apart from these official duties his position is, by immemorial tradition, one of

[1] B. H. Baden-Powell, *The Origin and Growth of Village Communities in India* (1899), p. 124.
[2] *Village Communities in the East and West* (1871), p. 12; *Ancient Law* (1891), p. 264.

honour to which certain privileges and some power are attached. The life of the village revolves round him and his presence is essential at certain ceremonies and festivals. In some places he has sacrificial functions very like those of the headman among aboriginal tribes: in parts of Berar, for example, he sacrifices a buffalo in the presence of all the villagers in order to ward off an epidemic of cholera, and at one of the great festivals when a buffalo is sacrificed to Durga, he makes the first cut, after which the Mahars finish off the animal.

The existence of headmen does not in any way preclude that of *panchayats*, which are found in *ryotwari* villages just as much as in joint villages: as has been pointed out by Baden-Powell, a *panchayat*, or committee of elders for settling disputes, is found in every form of village, whether in the north or south, and quite independently of what the village constitution is. It does not, however, merely settle disputes, but discusses and decides matters of common interest to the villagers, such as the allotment of facilities for irrigation to different villagers and the management and audit of the village fund.

There is a conflict of opinion as to the origin of the *ryotwari* or severalty village. One view, advanced by Mr. Baden-Powell, is that it is of tribal origin, villages being formed by sections of tribes, each under a leader, who allotted land to different families of settlers and became the village headman. This, as will be seen from the account given in Chapters III and IV, is the form of village prevalent among non-Aryan tribes, to whom the idea of a village without a headman seems scarcely conceivable. Another view is put forward by Mr. J. D. Mayne, who states that in Western and Central India the wars and devastations of Moslems, Marathas, and Pindaris swept away the village institutions as well as almost every other form of ancient proprietary right, while in Madras, where each occupant is separately liable for the land revenue, and not the whole village, the contrary usage must, in his opinion, once have existed.[1]

This latter view is supported by Sir Paul Vinogradoff, who attributes the disappearance of the joint village to the steam-roller effect of oppressive government. The *pattidari* type of village, he says, bears the stamp of the greater antiquity, and the *ryotwari* villages 'are nothing but casual concentrations of individuals: the population has been pulverized into a number of separate units by the grinding-powers of the *rajas* and their tax-gatherers. . . . It is not from the exploited subjects of the Moghuls or of the Mahrattas that the students of social origins can derive information about the beginnings of land tenure.'[2]

It is not proposed to enter into this controversy. There can be no doubt as to the way in which misrule can be a solvent of proprietary rights. To cite a comparatively modern instance, shortly after the annexation of the Punjab, Sikh cultivators, when questioned by an English officer as to their pre-existing rights of property, used to reply 'Why ask such a question? It is you who have created property'; while Sir Donald McLeod, Lieutenant-Governor of the Punjab, reported in 1866: 'The state of things existing in the Punjab for a long series of years preceding annexation was such as almost to extinguish proprietary rights in land or at all events to deprive them of nearly all their value.' The extinction of rights in property is, however, not the same thing as the extinction of village institutions—in the Punjab the indigenous system of village government retained its vitality, even when the people possessed only indistinct ideas as to their rights. It also may be doubted whether the Moghul Government interfered with the interior economy of villages so long as their revenue demands were met, and it is noticeable that *ryotwari* villages are found

---

[1] *Hindu Law* (9th edition), ch. vii, § 222.
[2] *Historical Jurisprudence* (1920), vol. i, p. 325.

in parts of South India which were not brought under direct Moghul rule or Maratha dominion, while the *pattidari* villages are found in the area which was longest under Moghul rule and which was not immune from the ravages of the Marathas.

Village communities of the *ryotwari* type prevail in Madras, Bombay, and the Central Provinces, and formerly existed in Bengal and Bihar. In the latter two areas they have died out, largely as a result of the creation of a landlord class by the Permanent Settlement of 1793 and the dominating influence of the landlords. There are men still bearing the old designations of village headmen, but they are no longer village officers representing the villagers in their dealings with outside authorities, but servants of the landlords, by whom they are paid and whose orders they carry out. The same has been the fate of the village accountants, who still keep up registers of holdings but merely as agents of the landlords. Practically the only trace of the old village community is the existence of village artisans and menials, who are still largely remunerated for their services by the traditional payments in kind. Attempts have been made to revive the village system by means of legislation, which has created boards elected by the villagers themselves for the management of village affairs, but these are purely administrative bodies of artificial creation and not part of the old indigenous system.

It may well be asked at this stage why the village of either class should be known as a village community, why, for instance, Mountstuart Elphinstone described it as in many respects an organized commonwealth complete within itself, while Lord Metcalfe said that each formed a separate little state, a little republic having nearly everything it could want within itself. One reason is that at the time they wrote village self-government was more complete and effective than it now is; in the intervening century it has been weakened by the

centralization of administrative authority, by the police and
revenue systems, and by the influence of the law-courts.
Another reason is that when communications were few and
bad, each village was a self-contained and independent economic unit. The villagers raised their own crops and lived
on them; subsidiary needs, such as oil, cloth, tools, pots and
pans, &c., were met by craftsmen attached to the village, who
worked not for individual villagers as a matter of contract,
but for the whole body of villagers. They were, and still are,
consequently known as village servants and were remunerated
either by small holdings, called service holdings, or by prescribed shares of the crop which they took at the time of
harvest, e.g. at the rate of so many sheaves of rice or other
grain per acre; or they might be remunerated by a combination
of both. There were other village servants who rendered
personal service, such as barbers, washermen, and menials,
all of whom received customary allowances. On the menials
the sanitation of the village depended, for they were scavengers
and they removed the carcases of dead animals, getting the
hides as a perquisite. In all cases there was an absence of the
competitive system, the village servants working for their own
village and not for a larger market, and as they were paid in
kind, their prosperity depended on that of the agricultural
community for which they worked.

Each village made its own arrangements for the maintenance
of rights in land, having for this purpose a village accountant,
who kept up the village accounts and a register in which were
recorded particulars of each holding. He is still the most
important functionary next to the headman, for he is called
in by the villagers to help them in anything requiring education and brains. The village also had its own establishment for
the preservation of law and order. In other words, it had a
watchman or watchmen according to its size. The latter was
very often a member of a caste of criminal propensities, and

was employed partly on the principle of setting a thief to catch a thief and partly with the idea that his employment was a kind of pledge for the good behaviour of his fellows.

In some parts there is a village servant whose special duty it is to attend to the supply of water from the irrigation channels to the fields and to see that each man gets his due turn. In Madras he calculates the time required for each by methods primitive to the point of quaintness. One is by measuring his shadow; the other is not quite so simple. The water measurer has a brass bowl or cup in the bottom of which a minute hole is bored. This is floated on a pot of water, and fills and sinks in twenty minutes, which is the time sufficient to irrigate about two-thirds of an acre: there are marks on the inside to show when it is a quarter, half, or three-quarters full.[1]

Various other persons were required for religious and social purposes, such as temple priests and, in the less civilized villages, priests to propitiate various deities, mostly of a malignant character, whom Brahmanism did not recognize. The number and duties of these officers varied very much. Some were of a quaint character, such as astrologers, bards, and, in Central India, wizards of two kinds: one charmed away tigers from the villagers and their cattle; another had the magic power of averting hailstorms from the young crops. Astrologers and bards and genealogists are still fairly common. The bard recites the genealogies of the hosts at feasts, especially wedding feasts. The astrologer is closely connected with family and agricultural life. He draws up horoscopes on which the choice of brides and bridegrooms largely depends, and he announces what days are auspicious or inauspicious for marriages and also for the commencement of ploughing, sowing, and harvesting.

The organization of the villages as separate self-sufficing industrial units was a natural consequence of the almost com-

[1] F. J. Richards, *Salem District Gazetteer* (Madras, 1918), pp. 236-7, 290.

plete absence of roads and the unsettled condition of the country.
In many parts the villages still nestle under the forts or within
the walls built to protect them against raids: in Berar the
village forts are often 30 feet high and so large that the whole
population with its herds could take refuge in them. Their
isolation has only been broken down during the last seventy
years. It is not always realized that the present network of
roads, as well as of railways, is of quite recent creation. 'Even
an enlightened man like Sir Charles Metcalfe', writes Sir John
Strachey, 'could maintain in 1830 that India required no
roads; and in fact there were none.'[1] Nor was there much
improvement till after the Mutiny and the transfer of the
government of India to the Crown. In Southern Oudh there
are said to have been not even fifty carts before the Mutiny,
all traffic was carried by pack bullocks, ponies, and coolies,
and there were not even cart-tracks.[2] In a Bihar district of
4,700 square miles, which is now cut up by railways and roads,
the District Officer, when a requisition was made on him for
transport during the Mutiny, reported that pack-bullocks were
the only means of transport, and, as he could get no carts, he
had to make them.

Under such conditions the villages were independent of the
outside world for the necessities of life except as regards a few
articles like salt. The cultivators lived on the crops which they
raised, the village servants, who received shares of the produce
or fixed allowances in kind, were equally dependent on them.
Village did not compete with village for the command of markets, nor was there competition between either skilled or un-
skilled labourers. As the villagers did not require outside help,
there was little migration from place to place. The cultivators
tilled the same lands as their ancestors, the village servants were

[1] *India: Its Administration and Progress* (1911), p. 231.
[2] Sir George Campbell, *Memoirs of my Indian Career* (1893), vol. ii,
p. 32.

descendants of men who had worked for the cultivators' ancestors, and the hereditary relations of the two classes remained unchanged from generation to generation.

Since the country has been opened up by roads, railways, and latterly the motor-bus, the villages are no longer isolated and self-supporting to the same extent. Local produce is exported: imported goods have found their way to rural areas, where they compete with local products. Greater facilities of communication and the possibilities of more profitable employment elsewhere have made labour less stationary and more mobile. Some village handicrafts have been practically killed by the competition of imports, in particular weaving and the manufacture of oil. Machine-made piece goods have supplanted the cloths woven on hand-looms, and kerosene oil the vegetable oil produced by village oilmen, so that both weavers and oilmen have had to take to other pursuits. Some villages have been changed almost out of recognition because of the extension of the railway to them, or because of the establishment of industrial concerns in or near them, or because of their neighbourhood to towns. In consequence of the increase of population which has followed their development hereditary artisans no longer suffice for their needs. Outsiders have been introduced who are alien to the old social constitution, and the competitive system takes the place of hereditary service.

The change has gone very far in some areas. In one district, for instance (Amraoti in Berar), it is said that little remains of the old village community except the headman, the village accountant, and the menial servants. Those handicraftsmen who were paid by customary allowances of shares in the crops are no longer so paid. The village blacksmith has become a stamp-vendor or publican, the tailor speculates in cotton, the pots made by the potter have given place to kerosene oil tins. Some of the village servants connected with social or religious life still, however, survive: the astrologer subsists on his hereditary piece of land; the hail wizard gets a precarious living from the credulous; the drummers who constitute the village band are still in request at family ceremonies.[1]

In areas such as these the village community is being so far modified to suit new conditions, that it may be said to be in a state of economic transition. The village artisans are beginning to be the creatures of contract rather than of status, i.e. instead of being the servants of the whole village with a yearly wage paid in kind, they work for individual employers and they are paid by the job and not necessarily in kind. The industrial organization of the village is, however, only a part of a whole, and other parts remain with little change.

The effects of the spread of communications and the development of trade and industries are, moreover, not so widespread as they might at first sight appear to be. Industrialized areas are few in number, and as has been pointed out in a recent blue book of the Government of India, even now, despite the remarkable improvements in communications which have taken place, only a small proportion of the hundreds of thousands of villages have either railways or metalled roads within several miles of them. Access to the great majority is obtained by pathways between the fields and rough cart-tracks, which are impracticable for wheeled traffic during the rainy season. Such villages are still to a large extent isolated and economically self-sufficing.

'Throughout the greater part of the country the typical self-contained Indian village community, which has been maintained unmodified for centuries, still exists—an interesting and surprisingly intricate social organism, in many ways resembling the characteristic rural unit of which we read in histories of mediaeval Europe, and containing its land-holders and tenants and agricultural labourers, its priest and its religious mendicant, its

[1] *Amraoti District Gazetteer* (Nagpur, 1911), pp. 148–57.

money-lender, and a whole order of artisans—the carpenter, the blacksmith, and the weaver, the potter and the oil-presser— each with his clearly prescribed functions hallowed by centuries of tradition.'[1]

To this general account may be added a sketch of life in typical villages of South India, which will serve to show the general working of the village system there.

'The small communities which inhabit the villages possess in themselves almost all the elements which should go to form a strong corporate spirit: a common temple and a *choultry*[2] in which the villagers collect and gossip, a village watch, and a company of artisans, to whose support every one makes a rateable contribu- tion, pasture-grounds, cattle-yards, and threshing-floors common to all, and often tanks and channels in the maintenance of which almost all alike have an interest. Sometimes there are village funds derived from the proceeds of communal lands or from the annual sale of the right to the fishery of the tank and from trees which are jointly owned by the whole community. In a few villages funds of comparatively recent origin are raised by pro- portionate contributions from all the land-owners. The money raised by these various methods is spent on the clearing of tanks and channels, the purchase and distribution of manure, the support of temple festivals, the feeding of travellers, and some- times, it is to be feared, in securing the favour of the lower ranks of officials.'[3]

But, the writer of this account adds, the average village scarcely possesses the strength born of unity. Instead of corporate harmony, there is faction. Disputes are chronic, and they are settled in the law courts rather than in the village itself. The same state of discord is found in joint villages, where too the

---

[1] *Statement exhibiting the Moral and Material Progress of India during the year 1930–31* (1932), p. 155.
[2] A village hall, which may be a simple shed.
[3] H. R. Pate, *Trinevelly District Gazetteer* (Madras, 1917), p. 103.

law courts have undermined the authority of the *panchayats* and largely taken their place. Co-sharers are constantly quarrelling over money matters, the disposal of the common waste land, &c., and only too often they have their differences settled by the law courts rather than by the local *panchayats*, whose decisions have no finality and can be upset by legal process.

VI

THE FAMILY

WHILE the village is the communal unit, the family may be described as the fundamental unit, of Hindu society. It is the most closely knit of the group units of Indian society because of the intimacy of the connexion between its members and the strong sense of community of blood. Just as there are joint villages and 'severalty' villages, so there are joint families and separate families, one having common property and living together, while in the other the members have separate property and separate establishments. Among Hindus, however, separate families are merely the product of the joint family, which is an archaic form of social organization, the structure of which shows a stage of development which has long ago been passed in Europe.

'The primitive ideas of mankind were unequal to comprehending any basis of the connexion *inter se* of individuals apart from the relations of family. The family consisted primarily of those who belonged to it by consanguinity and next of those who had been engrafted on it by adoption.'[1] Sir Henry Maine's description of the early type of family applies precisely to the Hindu family of to-day, which not only consists of blood relations but may also include adopted sons. In other countries the custom of adoption is generally resorted to in order to perpetuate a family. In India the main motive is religious. A Hindu can only attain salvation after death and ensure that of his ancestors by means of offerings made by a son or a son's son or a son's son's son lawfully begotten in marriage. If there is no son to perform his funeral rites and make the due offerings, his spirit remains disembodied and in a state of misery. 'Heaven', says one text, 'is not for him who

[1] *Ancient Law* (1891), p. 165.

leaves no male progeny.' A son's offerings, however, ensure bliss for the uneasy spirit: the Sanskrit name of a son (*putra*) actually means one who delivers from hell. The birth of a son in marriage thus affects a man's immortal life besides carrying on the family line. An adopted son is just as efficacious an agent of salvation as a lawfully begotten son; offerings made by the former ensure salvation as fully as those made by the latter. It will readily be understood, therefore, why a man who has no son adopts one.

Adoption is the factitious creation of blood relationship, but it so closely resembles real kinship that no distinction is made, either in the eye of the law or in public opinion, between a real son and an adopted son. The adopted son is not merely a substitute for a real son in regard to funeral ceremonies: his adoption has more than a religious significance. He leaves his own family finally and for ever; he is as much a member of the new family as a real son, and he has the full rights of a son as regards property and inheritance.

Naturally an adopted son must be of the same caste as the adoptor, and the field of choice is further narrowed by a rule that he must not be the son of a woman whom the adoptor could not lawfully have married: the idea is that the adopted son must at least be a boy who might have been a real son. Naturally also an only son, though eligible, is rarely adopted, because he would cease to have the relationship of sonship to his own father, and a father is not likely to imperil his immortal soul by leaving himself without a son to make sacramental offerings for him. A man may, however, adopt his brother's only son because no change of family is involved. Such an adopted son is called 'the son of two fathers' (*dwyamushyayana*), and there is an express agreement between the fathers that his relationship to his natural family shall continue, so that he does not pass from one family to another but inherits in both.[1]

---

[1] When a man gives his only son in adoption to his brother, the courts,

Adoption should take place in the case of the twice-born castes before a boy assumes the sacred thread, i.e. while he is still of tender years, but in the case of the lower castes it should take place before his marriage. A man can authorize his wife or his widow to adopt a son, and this authority is frequently exercised by the widow if he happens to die without a son, in order that the necessary offerings may be made for his spirit. So essential is it that there should be a son to act as the saviour of a man's soul, that even if he has not expressly authorized his widow to adopt, she is allowed to do so after his death in South and West India. In the south the sanction of his relatives is required; in West India even that formality is dispensed with and his consent to her action is presumed. Elsewhere a widow cannot adopt without the specific permission of her husband in consequence of a text which lays down that a woman should neither give nor accept a son without the assent of her lord. By adopting a son, a widow loses her right to her husband's estate, which *ipso facto* vests in the adopted son (subject to her right of maintenance), so that she may be regarded as sacrificing her material interests for the spiritual benefit of her late husband.

The Hindu joint family system is a survival of the time when social ties were based on consanguinity in the male, and not the female, line. It is still of the utmost importance as a social institution, for it is the foundation of the Hindu law of ownership and succession. The members of a family under this system must be males who are descended from a common ancestor in the male line, or who have been given that position by adoption, together with their wives and unmarried daughters. The prefix unmarried will be noted. A daughter on

except in Bombay, presume that the adoption was made in this special form unless it is proved that the adoption was in the ordinary form. In Bombay, on the other hand, it is presumed that the adoption was in the ordinary form unless it is proved that there was an agreement that the boy was to be 'the son of two fathers'.

marriage is cut off from her father's family and becomes a member of her husband's family. 'With us', writes Mr. Yusuf Ali, 'the daughter is not the daughter all the days of her life: she is only the daughter *until* she is a wife. Then she enters into a new circle and new relationships, and she literally worships a new set of gods.'[1] A family consequently is reduced in numbers by the loss of daughters or sisters, who go off to other families, and is increased by the accession of the married women whom it receives and absorbs.

In its complete form a joint family has a common property, a common house, with a common kitchen and common worship of a family idol or idols. If all the members of the family live together, the establishment is often more like a colony than a household. There may, for example, be a man and his wife, his brothers and their wives, his sons and their wives, his grandsons and their wives. There may be as many as four generations all living under one roof, and the total number of persons may run to one hundred and even to hundreds, though such large numbers are far rarer than they used to be. Some fifty years ago it was estimated that one particular family included 500 persons;[2] in another joint family as many as 91 women have actually been enumerated.[3] Such large numbers combined with the purdah system require large convent-like mansions in towns and a number of straggling buildings in villages, where land is cheaper and new buildings are easily added.

It must not be concluded that all members of the family reside together. The conditions of modern life often prevent this, as men have to go away for professional and other work in towns and cities, the management of business, &c. But there is a home in which the worship of the family idol is kept

---

[1] *Life and Labour of the People of India* (1907), p. 273.
[2] S. C. Bose, *The Hindus as they are* (1881), p. 2.
[3] W. E. S. Holland, *The Goal of India* (1918), p. 100.

up, in which every member of the family has a right to live, and in which there is a more or less complete family gathering on the occasion of certain festivals. In any case, the women and children usually remain there if the men's work calls them away, and one or more male members of the family stay at home to look after them. Hindus are warmly attached to this family home—'the ancestral home' as it is called in Bengal —both for reasons of natural sentiment and also because it is associated with the family worship of the tutelary god. When a family is broken up by partition of the estate, and the property is divided among the different members, arrangements are very frequently made for the continuance of the family worship. If this is not done and there is only one idol, it is sometimes sent round to the members of the disjointed family in turn, so that each has what is called a turn of worship.

Besides having a right to reside in the family house, every member of the family has a right to the enjoyment of the family property, whether he contributes to it or not. All things are enjoyed in common. There is one common fund from which the common expenses are met and into which are paid the sums received from all earning members, including remittances from absent members. No one is compelled to contribute to the common stock, and some take an unfair advantage of their liberty. Those who are constitutionally lazy or parasitical are content to live in idleness without making an effort to earn enough for their support. Family drones are the curse of the joint family. All money earned by means of the family property must be paid into the common fund; but anything which a man makes by his own personal exertions without drawing on the family funds remains exclusively his personal property, and the family has no claim on it; it has been provided by a recent Act, the Gains of Learning Act, passed in 1930, that property acquired by means of education provided at the expense of the family funds is no longer to be regarded as joint family property, but is the exclusive and separate property of the person who acquires it. Besides this, the wedding gifts, jewelry, ornaments, &c., which a bride brings with her on marriage, and presents which she may receive subsequently, are her exclusive property.

The property which is held in common is administered by a manager, who is generally the eldest male. As manager, he simply represents the family, from which his powers are derived and to which he is responsible as a trustee. Actually he possesses great authority both because he is the head of the family and because of the reverence paid to age and experience. The purely domestic matters of the household do not come within his domain. In these the senior woman of the family reigns supreme and her authority extends to social matters as she regards herself as the custodian of the family honour.

Except in Bengal, where the father has special rights, the property of the family, which is governed by what is called Mitakshara law, belongs not to any individual person or persons, but to all the male members of the family in commonalty, the family being a sort of corporation. Women are regarded as mere dependants of their fathers or husbands and have no part or lot in ownership, as apart from the enjoyment of the property and a right to be maintained out of it while they continue in the family. Ownership is corporate and is not affected by the death of any member of the family. As soon as he is born, every male child acquires a vested interest in the ancestral property, becoming a co-owner with his father, brothers, and other male relatives. He is entitled to a specific share of the property and can become a separate owner of it only if and when the family ceases to be joint and the property is partitioned. No part of the property can be alienated without the common consent, actual or presumed, of all the members of the family.

Bengal is under a different system of law called Dayabhaga,

according to which a family which has a common ancestor (such as a grandfather or father) alive, has common enjoyment of the property but not common rights of ownership. The common ancestor is not only the manager but the owner of the property with a right to dispose of it during his lifetime. Sons and grandsons become co-owners only on his death. Each of them is then owner of a definite though undivided share, which he may dispose of if he likes. It can be separated from the rest of the property if one of them desires separate enjoyment; otherwise the property will remain joint. There are consequently two kinds of joint family—one under the common ancestor, who is sole owner, the other consisting of brothers and their descendants, each of whom is owner of, and free to dispose of, his undivided share.

The maintenance of the joint family depends on the continued consent of the members,[1] who to an increasing extent prefer separation. Formerly the joint family was rarely dissolved on the death of a father, and continued joint for several generations, but such cases are now the exception and not the rule. The economic conditions of modern life and the working of the leaven of new ideas are common causes of partition. Men no longer live at home in their native villages to anything like the former extent, but obtain employment elsewhere. Their separation from the home life may be temporary but is often permanent, and is not uncommonly a prelude to the separation of their shares.

Again, men and women imbued with new ideas chafe under the restraints of the old conventional life usually led in conservative Hindu homes. Mutual friction results, which may become intolerable as, for example, when some of the family are orthodox Hindus who keep up traditional customs and

---

[1] A son can require a partition of the ancestral property even during his father's lifetime, but this is looked upon with disfavour, and it is usual for a discontented son to wait till his father's death.

others have abandoned them: one case is known of a family being broken up because a man was determined to give his daughter an English education, to which his relations objected.

Family disputes are the most usual cause of the dissolution of families into separate branches. In particular, earning members who contribute to the family resources are disgusted by a system under which idle relatives are a drain upon them, and their wives, devoted to their husbands' interests, keenly resent their energies being exploited. Or there may be actual mismanagement of the property and possible malversation of funds by the manager, both of which are a legitimate ground for separation. Less worthy motives are not absent. Family factions are produced by petty quarrels and jealousies; wives are said to be especially disruptive of the joint family life. A contributory, but by no means negligible, factor is the decay in the upper castes of the *panchayats* which formerly settled many family disputes and so prevented dismemberment. Nowadays members of a family who are at loggerheads do not seek their aid but put themselves in a lawyer's hands. Litigation ensues, feelings are embittered, and mutual estrangement ends in splitting up the family.

Sometimes the members of a family will live in separate households but keep the property intact, dividing the proceeds, such as rents from lands and the profits of business, between themselves according to their respective shares. Even after the family is broken up, the ancestral home is not necessarily abandoned. The family may continue to live in the same house or homestead as a matter of cheapness and convenience, but its members will live apart in their own sets of rooms or in separate buildings, having, if possible, a separate entrance, and each maintaining a separate domestic budget. Dwelling-houses may be occupied, particularly in towns and cities, by three or four separate families, each of which shuts off the apartments in which it lives by means of partition walls, both because of the seclusion demanded by purdah (among the upper classes) and because of mutual bad feeling. The result too frequently is that a fine mansion with spacious courtyards is converted into a number of mean little houses with totally inadequate lighting and ventilation, and cases are known in which an unfortunate householder can only reach his own part of the house through a long tortuous passage.

It is not possible to estimate the extent to which the joint family system is being given up, but special inquiries which were made in Bihar and Orissa during the census of 1911 show that it continues only in a minority of cases. It was estimated that not more than one in every four families in Bihar, and only one in every five in Orissa, continued joint after the death of parents. The disruption might take place after a father's death or, if he left a widow, be deferred until after the mother's death, but in the majority of cases it was deferred no longer, and it was rare to find a family which remained undivided for two generations or more. The fissiparous tendency is strongest among the professional and mercantile classes and weakest among the agricultural classes, both because of their ingrained conservatism and because a joint family which has able-bodied men to work on the land can more easily dispense with hired labour.

The breaking up of joint families does not involve the entire abandonment of the joint family system, because each son on taking his separate share starts a new joint family with his sons. The family, it is true, may consist only of a man, his wife, and his children, but it is still a joint family, for the sons have equal rights with their father to shares in the family property. The general effect is that large joint families are replaced by small joint families, many in number and short in duration. Practically the only case in which a single individual is sole owner is when a man is the only surviving member of a joint family to whom the property has passed by right of sole survivorship;

and if on his death the property passes to the head of a family, it again becomes joint property.

The decline of the joint family system is not to be regretted, for it belongs to an earlier stage of social growth. It has admittedly some admirable traits. It forms a strong bond of union between relations and promotes family solidarity: its keynote is 'All for each and each for all'. It ensures protection for the weaker sex, particularly widows, provides support for the aged and infirm, and is an insurance against unemployment: it is to some extent due to the existence of the joint family system that India has been able to do without a Poor Law system. It fosters discipline because individual interests have to be subordinated to those of the family. It encourages unselfishness and generosity: it is regarded as natural that poor relations should have a claim on their kith and kin. An Indian family has little of the uncharitable and snobbish feeling about poor relations which we find, for example, in Charles Lamb's long list of opprobrious similes, such as a death's head at your banquet, a Lazarus at your door, a fly in your ointment, a triumph to your enemies, and an apology to your friends.

On the other hand, the system discourages independence and initiative, besides giving a loop-hole for idleness, if it does not actually put a premium on it. It limits liberty of action to such an extent that a man may be said to lead not his own life but the life of his family. He must subscribe to its canons of conduct and submit to its regimentation of duties: the family is everything, the individual nothing. The concentration of authority in the head of the family, while making for discipline, reverence for age, and obedience, may be an unhealthy influence, for junior members live in a state of subordination which obscures personal responsibility and prevents development of character. This is especially marked in the case of women. As pointed out by Mrs. Sarangadhar Das in *Purdah*, the mother, or in her absence, the wife of the eldest male member, is the virtual ruler of the household. 'She is the one final granite stronghold of orthodoxy and preserver of outworn customs, and for a little daughter-in-law to defy her is almost unthinkable. Every female member is bound to implicit obedience to all her regulations, directions, or orders. These extend not only to household matters but even to the daughter-in-law's intimate relations with her own husband and children.'

The joint family also creates conditions favourable to early marriage, whereas its dissolution tends to raise the age of marriage. So long as it endures there is no question of a young husband being unable to support a wife. He need not leave his parental home and set up house for himself; the family will support him and his wife; and a youth need not therefore wait till he is in a position to earn an independent livelihood. On the other hand, early marriage is not so easy if there is no joint family. Young men have to wait till they earn enough to set up house and to support their wives, added to which they want wives who are not mere children but are capable of managing their homes properly. .

The traditional type of family among Moslems is one of a patriarchal character united both by kinship and by obedience to a common head, generally the oldest member. Patriarchal authority has, however, been undermined. The word of the head of the family is no longer law to its younger members, who set up separate establishments, and the modern family tends to consist merely of a man, his wife, and children. Moreover, the Islamic law on the subject of maintenance and inheritance is not, like the Hindu law, a factor in favour of joint estates; incidentally it does not, like the Hindu law, recognize adoption as a source of rights. It regards property as essentially individual and is not based on the idea of a joint estate to be maintained for the common needs of a family. Besides this, a man is not obliged to maintain either his sons, when adult or able-bodied, or his daughters, when married; and 'there is

nothing to suggest or encourage the keeping of a family
together after the death of its head'.[1]

The agricultural tribes of the Punjab observe their own
tribal law and follow neither Islamic nor canonical Hindu law
in matters affecting the family property. Many of them are
known to have been originally Hindus who embraced Islam
to save their ancestral land. The alternative being Islam or
confiscation, they accepted Islam, but while they loosely
adhered to its creed, they never fully adopted its personal law
but retained the tribal law which they had before their change
of religion. Under Islamic law an estate on the death of
the owner is divided among different sharers, including
females, each of whom is entitled to absolute ownership of
his or her share; women do not lose their rights by marrying into another family as is the case with Hindus. Both the
Moslem and the Hindu tribes, on the contrary, base their
customary law on the principle of agnatic male succession,
with the right of ownership limited by the rights of agnates.

Among these tribes both Hindus and Moslems alike have
a joint family system which in some respects resembles that
governed by the Mitakshara law. The father is the head of the
family: sons acquire rights in the family property as soon as
they are born. Daughters have none, and are entitled only to
maintenance, but a widow without sons has an interest in the
property until her remarriage or death. The father cannot
alienate the property without the consent of the male agnates
who would naturally succeed him except in case of necessity,
e.g. to save the whole by selling a part. He is subject to their
control simply because the rule of agnatic succession would not
operate if he had absolute power of alienation. The whole
position is, as summarized in a judgement of the Senior Judge
of the Chief Court of the Punjab, that by customary law no

[1] Sir R. K. Wilson, *Introduction to the Study of Anglo-Muhammadan
Law* (1894), pp. 143–4.

individual, whether or not he has male issue, is under ordinary circumstances competent by his own sole act to prevent the devolution of ancestral land in accordance with the rules of succession, i.e. upon his male descendants in the male line, if any, or failing them upon his agnate kinsmen in order of proximity. The exercise of any power which would affect the operation of these rules to the detriment of the natural successors to ancestral land is liable to be controlled by them whether the act done be a partition, or a gift, or a sale or mortgage otherwise than for necessity or an adoption.[1]

Adoption among the Punjab tribes is practised only by those which are of Hindu origin and differs from adoption as sanctioned by Hindu law because it has no religious significance. The person adopted must be one of the agnatic heirs, and the object of adoption is simply to preserve the ancestral land in the male agnate line. If, as rarely happens, a widow adopts, she also must adopt a near agnate relative of her late husband and must have the consent of the other agnates. Adoption cannot be made privately as under Hindu law; to ensure validity it must be publicly notified before the assembled brotherhood.

It is not possible to generalize about such a miscellaneous set of communities as the non-Aryan tribes, but it is noticeable that a type of family resembling in some ways the joint family is found among various non-Aryan tribes of the interior, such as the Mundas, Santals, Khonds, and Oraons. It is customary for the whole family, including sons, their wives, and grandchildren, to live together in the cluster of buildings making up the homestead and for all to acknowledge the patriarchal authority of the father or common ancestor, who is its head. All toil in the fields together, all share common meals, all contribute to a common fund, which often merely means that their earnings and savings are put into a common jar or pot,

[1] C. A. Roe and H. A. B. Rattigan, *Tribal Law in the Punjab* (Lahore, 1895), pp. 20, 21, 26, and 83.

from which money is drawn out to meet common expenses. The family shares all that it has in common until the father's death, when the property is divided according to the customary tribal law. Both movable and immovable property is divided among the sons in equal shares, except that the eldest may get a little more than his brothers, say an extra field or bullock, or a little extra money; among both the Mundas and Oraons, even if a son has emigrated, he retains his right to a share in the ancestral property, but not in the family savings unless he has remitted money home. Daughters have properly no right of succession, but if a man dies without sons, they may be allowed to keep possession of his land until they die or marry. Sons have no right to a partition during their father's lifetime, but he himself sometimes partitions the property, as for instance when he makes a second marriage, keeping one share for himself and giving each of his sons one. The father has certain independent powers, e.g. among the Mundas he can expel a son for disobedience, and the son thereby forfeits his right to a share in the property, or he may make a son live separately with a share of which he determines the amount. Generally speaking, his power to dispose of property is limited by the rights of those who are entitled to succeed to it on his death under the customary law of the tribe, and any disposition of it contrary to that law would be invalid.

Neither Hindu nor Islamic nor tribal law admits of rights of primogeniture, and sons obtain equal shares. Under the Hindu and tribal law of succession property is divided among sons or agnates, while Islamic law involves a complicated and often minute system of subdivision. The rules of succession have resulted in an extreme fragmentation of holdings of land, which has affected the agricultural economy of the country. Large holdings are reduced to small, and even fields are split up into plots, becoming more and more minute—a phenomenon often described by the use of French terms such as *morcellement* of land and *petite culture*, which is characteristic both of French and Indian agriculture and is due to similar causes.[1] The average size of the holdings is not more than 5 acres in South and East India; in other parts of the country half of the holdings are no larger, and many are as small as an acre or even less. The result of such minute subdivision of property, combined with the growth of population, is that many are unable to get a living from the land and the number of landless labourers seeking employment outside their own villages is on the increase.

Another distinguishing feature of the family both among Hindus and non-Aryan tribes is that it is patriarchal in type in so far as it is governed by the father and not the mother, while there is agnatic male succession, women being in a subordinate position as dependants of their husbands and fathers. There are some exceptions to this general rule, for matriarchy is found in a few communities, i.e. family property and relationship are concentrated round the mother, not the father, and descent is reckoned, and property passes, in the female and not in the male line. This is the system observed by the Khasis of Assam, among whom, as stated at the end of Chapter III, the mother is the head of the family; the children belong to her clan and not their father's clan, and inheritance is transmitted through her. It is also common in Malabar and Travancore, where it is followed by Nairs (or Nayars) and other castes but not by Brahmans. It is known in that part of the country by a name meaning 'descent through a sister's children', which exactly expresses it, for a man's heirs are not his own sons (who belong to their mother's family and not his) but his sister's sons. Succession to the rulership of Travancore follows this rule, so that a Maharaja is succeeded by his sister's

---

[1] Under the French law of succession a father's testamentary power to dispose of property is limited to a part equal to the share of one child; the rest is divided equally among his children.

son. In order that the line of rulers may be continued girls are said to be desired as ardently as sons are by Hindus in other parts of India. If there is no girl in the family or no prospect of one, the Maharaja adopts girls from collateral families. The present Maharaja owes his position to the adoption of his mother. In 1900 the late Maharaja adopted two girls, of whom one became the Senior Maharani and had no sons, while the other, who became the Junior Maharani, had two sons. On the death of the Maharaja in 1924 the eldest of these boys was proclaimed Maharaja of Travancore and, as he was a minor, the Senior Maharani, according to old custom, became Maharani-Regent.

The joint family in Malabar consists of the descendants of a common ancestress in the female line. Its property is the common property of all the members, all of whom are entitled to maintenance from it. None of them has a right to claim partition, but a partition may be effected by their common consent. It is usually managed by the eldest male member, who has practically absolute power over it and, unless he voluntarily resigns, can only be removed from his office on the ground of mismanagement or malversation by a decree of the Civil Court. Each member has a right to own and dispose of self-acquired property, but any that a man has not disposed of by gift or will lapses to the joint family on his death. A man may even use his self-acquired property to make a separate home for his wife and children, and such a household is a branch of the joint family and entitled to share in its joint property. There is a growing tendency for the more well-to-do to set up separate households of this kind; and each of them tends to become the nucleus of a fresh joint family, in which, as in the parent family, descent is traced in the female line.

VII

MARRIAGE

MARRIAGE is regarded by the great majority of Hindus as both a sacrament and a religious duty. According to the tenets of Hinduism it is incumbent on a man to marry so that he may beget a son who will make the offerings necessary for his salvation after death and for that of his ancestors. It is equally incumbent on parents to get their daughters married: by immemorial custom an unmarried daughter of marriageable age is a shame and a reproach to the family. Boys and girls are, therefore, commonly, though by no means universally, married at an age when they are unable to understand the meaning of marriage. This means that they go through a marriage ceremony, and not that they live together as man and wife. After the ceremony the bridegroom returns to his home and his girl-wife remains in hers until she has attained puberty, which is generally about the age of 11 or 12. The marriage is consummated at varying periods after that, and generally the period is all too short, as it is desired to have a son as soon as possible so as to ensure against an early death. In 1929 it was estimated by the Age of Consent Committee that nearly one-half of the girls of India were married before the age of fifteen, and it was stated that 'in some parts cohabitation often takes place before the child-wife has reached the age of puberty, and almost always very soon after'.

Marriage has no religious sanction for Moslems, but is a civil contract, and Moslem girls generally remain unmarried till some years after puberty, though some of the lower and more ignorant classes are so far infected by Hindu practices that they celebrate marriages for young children. A father, and failing him a grandfather, may arrange for the marriage of a girl while still a minor, and this agreement or contract is

carried out when she is of marriageable age, as either has
authority to act for her. Failing either the father or grandfather, a girl's brothers and certain other members of her
family can arrange for her marriage, but in that case the agreement is provisional, for the minor has the right to repudiate it
on attaining puberty. If the girl wishes to repudiate it, she
must do so immediately on attaining puberty: otherwise her
consent is presumed, and her right to repudiate is lost. The
boy, on the other hand, retains the right of repudiation until
he has ratified the agreement either expressly or implicitly,
as by payment of dower or cohabitation. In any case, the
girl has no opportunity of getting to know her prospective
bridegroom beforehand, for she does not see him before the
marriage takes place, and can only rely on outside information
or gossip.

The personal law of the Shias, who are only a small minority
in India, recognizes a temporary marriage, called *mutah*, which
by the terms of the contract terminates at the end of a fixed
period, such as six months, but may be renewed by the consent
of both parties. Many Moslems condemn marriage of this
kind. One writer stigmatizes it as a licensed form of prostitution,[1] and readers of Morier's *Hajji Baba* will remember that
the *muti* is described as 'a class of females who generally were
the refuse of womankind—old widows and deserted wives—
who, rather than live under the opprobrium that single life
entails in our Mohamedan countries would put up with anything that came under the denomination of husband'.

Early marriage is exceptional both among the aboriginal
races of the interior and among the Mongolian tribes of the
frontier, whose view is that a wife should be old enough to
be a helpmeet to her husband. Even among the Hindus,
moreover, the custom is far from prevalent in some parts,
notably in South India, where the number of child wives

[1] S. Khuda Baksh, *Essays: Indian and Islamic* (1912), p. 264.

is comparatively small, and in Rajputana, where the Rajputs agreed many years ago to fix the minimum age for marriage at 14 for females and 18 for males. The number elsewhere is unfortunately all too large, and consummation is so little deferred that child-wives soon become child-mothers: the Telegraph Department realizes an appreciable sum every year from the telegrams sent by parents to their sons-in-law telling them that menstruation has begun and that they should not stand on the order of their coming, but come at once.

This regrettable practice does not appear to have scriptural authority. The Laws of Manu, the highest authority on Hindu social customs, while inculcating the early celebration of marriage, contemplate its consummation being deferred and even permit of a girl remaining single; it is better, it is said, that a girl, though marriageable, should stay at home till death than that she should be given in marriage to a bridegroom without good qualities. Unfortunately this injunction is generally ignored and parents as a general rule are convinced that their daughters must be married before puberty; one superstition is that if they fail in this duty, the girl's father, grandfather, and great-grandfather will be punished by being reincarnated as insects at their next rebirth.

There are notable exceptions to this general rule. Marriages of girls of mature age are common among the Sikhs of the Punjab and among the Kulin Brahmans of Bengal and the Nambudri Brahmans of South India. The late age of marriage is due among the Kulin Brahmans to the difficulty of obtaining husbands under the operation of the law of hypergamy, and among the Nambudri Brahmans it is the result of their peculiar marriage customs. Only the eldest son of a family marries within the caste while younger sons contract informal, but not irregular, unions with non-Brahman women. There is consequently a shortage of eligible husbands for the Nambudri Brahman girls, with the result that they marry late in life or not at all. The belief in the necessity of marriage is so strong, however, that if an adult woman dies without being married, a formal ceremony of marriage with the corpse is celebrated, a man being hired for the occasion to officiate as bridegroom. Pious frauds of a like kind are not infrequent. With the idea that a symbolical marriage may serve the purpose in default of a real marriage, girls in some castes, for whom their parents have been unable to obtain a husband before they are of marriageable age, go through a form of marriage to an arrow, a dagger, or a tree.

Early marriage is becoming less general among the educated classes owing partly to economic causes and partly to the spread of enlightened ideas. Many parents are no longer bound by the trammels of dogma, or are strong-minded enough to throw them aside. Knowing the suffering caused by premature motherhood, they absolutely refuse to allow their daughters to run the risk of it. Nor is the opposition limited to parents. Educated young men are unwilling to have child-wives with minds as undeveloped as their bodies, and want brides who are their intellectual equals. Their attitude, as previously stated, has been strengthened by the breaking up of the joint family system. This used to enable young wives to be supported by the family, but nowadays young men have to set up house for themselves far more frequently, and as a natural consequence require wives old enough for household management.

Economic pressure has perhaps done more to raise the age of marriage. The expense of marrying daughters has gone up enormously among the higher castes because of the narrow circle within which marriage is possible and the competitive prices which suitable bridegrooms can command, not to mention the costliness of the marriage festivities and of the entertainments necessary to social prestige. A father with several daughters may have to scrimp and save for years before he can accumulate sufficient funds for each of their marriages, and in the meantime they must perforce remain single.

Legislation is another contributory factor, though it is hard to estimate its effect. The Indian Penal Code of 1860 treated the consummation of marriage with a wife under 10 years of age as rape, and provided for its punishment accordingly. In 1892 the age of consent was raised to 12, in consequence of public opinion being aroused by a number of horrible cases in which child-wives between the ages of 10 and 12 had been either done to death, or crippled, or paralysed by their husbands in exercise of their marital rights. It is only right to add that it was found that this practice was rare outside Bengal, and that there it was followed only within a portion of the province and only by certain classes in that portion.

The Age of Consent Act applied only to British India, and the Indian States were slow to follow the lead given by the Government of India; but in 1894 the State of Mysore passed a Regulation prohibiting the marriage of a man of 50 or more with a girl under 14, but either such marriages are infrequent or it has not been enforced strictly, for there have been only 99 convictions under it in 20 years (1911–31). In 1904 the State of Baroda made a further advance by an Act (the Infant Marriages Prevention Act) which fixed the minimum age of marriage at 14 for girls and 16 for boys. Some exceptions were made for certain special cases of girls aged 9 to 12, while the Kadwa Kunbis, who periodically have mass marriages[1] of

---

[1] They celebrate marriages both in Baroda and the Central Provinces on a single day which is fixed by astrologers once in every nine, ten, or eleven years, when there is a general clearance of marriageable persons of either sex. Other communities have marriage years at similar long intervals. The Bharvads of Baroda have one every 12, 15, or 24 years and the Chettis of Madras one every 10 or 15 years. Among some castes in the Central Provinces families with a large number of children celebrate two or three marriages at the same time in order to reduce expense, and in such cases babies under a year old may be married. See *Census of India Report for 1911*, Part I, p. 258.

children, were allowed to celebrate them for boys of 8 and girls of 6. This Act has been enforced by means of prosecutions, the number of which shows that early marriages have not been given up: there were on the average 4,000 convictions annually between 1911 and 1921 and in the next decade 6,500. Thousands of marriages of girls under age have been celebrated because, rather than give up a traditional custom, parents preferred to risk the chance of being prosecuted and fined, regarding the fines as a part (and a small part at that) of the marriage expenses. It is pointed out in the Baroda Census Report for 1931 that, though the Act has been in existence since 1904, the annual average of offences against it increased till 1930 almost to the extent of proving that its provisions had almost ceased to have any effect in changing the social conduct of the people. It cannot be doubted, it is said, that the penal provisions were wholly ineffective, and the people looked upon the light fines imposed as only an added item to their marriage budget, until the amendment of the Act in 1928. The amendments, besides raising the age of consent to 14 for unmarried females and to 18 for unmarried males, provide that marriages are void if the age of either party is under 8, raise the maximum limit of fines from Rs. 50 to Rs. 500, and render persons abetting the marriage of any one under 8 years of age liable to imprisonment and fine.

In British India the age of consent was advanced to 13 in 1925, and in 1929 an Act was passed, entitled the Child Marriage Restraint Act, but more generally known as the Sarda Act after its mover, Haribilas Sarda, which prohibits and penalizes, without, however, invalidating the marriage of males under 18 and of females under 14. It provides that a male above 18 years of age and below 21 who contracts a 'child marriage', i.e. a marriage with a girl under 14 years of age, is punishable with a fine which may extend to Rs. 1,000 and is not liable to imprisonment in default of payment. A man over

21 years of age who contracts such a marriage is punishable with simple imprisonment which may extend to one month or with a fine which may extend to Rs. 1,000 or with both. The latter penalties are also prescribed for any person who performs, contracts, or directs a 'child marriage' unless he proves that he had reason to believe that the marriage was not a child marriage. It is too early yet to gauge the effect of this measure. In itself it was a great advance due to the working, among the more advanced sections of the community, of enlightened opinion and to the feelings of humanity which have been aroused by the pitiable sufferings caused by premature maternity. Time is needed for the development of a body of public opinion which will make its provisions fully operative, more especially as prosecutions depend on private initiative. In the meantime it will have to contend with the forces of ignorance and orthodoxy, added to the practical difficulty of proving age in a country where proper registers of birth are not kept up.

Already there has been a sequel to its enactment which shows on the one hand that there is a healthy respect for the law, but on the other that the people cling to their old ways. The Act did not come into force till six months after it was passed. In anticipation of its coming into effect a vast number, estimated at hundreds of thousands, of marriages of girls under 14 were celebrated; and more undoubtedly have since taken place. The census of 1931, which was held a year after the Act came into force, gave some extraordinary results, which were directly due to this briskness in the marriage market. According to the statistics of this census the married men in India outnumber the married women by 600,000—a figure which might at first sight suggest that the people are to some extent polyandrous. Such a supposition, however, is opposed to known facts and to the results of each previous census: in 1921 the number of married women was in excess by half a million, which is what one might expect in a country where polygamy is practised to a small extent. The reason for the change was simply that parents who had married their daughters below the permissible age lied in order to avoid any risk of a prosecution and described them as unmarried. The number of married women as disclosed by the census was therefore fictitiously small; but even so it has regretfully to be recorded that 12¼ million girls under the age of 15 were returned as married.

Moslem marriages are not complicated, like those of the Hindus, by elaborate rules as to consanguinity and affinity. The table of prohibited degrees is much the same as that of Christians, and if a Moslem indulges in polygamy, his choice of wives is to some extent limited by affinity, e.g. he may not have two sisters, or an aunt and niece, as co-wives. He may, however, marry two sisters successively; he can espouse a deceased wife's sister and is also permitted to marry the widow of a deceased brother. Marriages of men are also not entirely confined to co-religionists, for a man may marry a Jewish or a Christian woman, as Jews and Christians are not idolaters, but people of the Book (i.e. the Bible); a Moslem woman, however, should marry only a Moslem.

The case is very different with Hindus, for marriage is hedged round by restrictions imposed by rules not only as to consanguinity, but also, according to the caste, by rules as to endogamy, i.e. marrying within a certain circle, exogamy, i.e. marrying outside a certain circle, and hypergamy, i.e. marrying into a circle of superior status. The general rule is that a man must marry a woman of his own caste or tribe. Further, it is a rule of most castes that the woman must belong to the same sub-caste. Inside the sub-castes there are further rules as to agnatic relationship which limits the circle within which marriage is permissible. A member of one of the twice-born castes may not marry within the same *gotra*, i.e. within a group which consists of persons descended from the same ancestor through an uninterrupted line of males. Yet another rule, which is called the rule of *sapinda* exogamy, narrows the marriage circle still farther, for it excludes cognates as well as agnates by prohibiting the marriage of a man with a woman descended from his paternal or maternal ancestors within the sixth or fourth degree respectively. The rigidity of this rule is relaxed by a proviso that, if a suitable marriage cannot otherwise be arranged, a man may marry a girl within the fifth degree on the father's side and within the third degree on the mother's side. It scarcely needs explaining that the result is a formidable list of prohibited degrees.

These rules are observed by the castes which subscribe to Brahmanical canons, particularly in North India. They are not in force among the lower castes of South India, which recognize the marriages of cousins as lawful and even expedient. Marriage with the daughter of a maternal uncle is most in favour, and next to that marriage with the daughter of a paternal aunt. A man is considered to have a preferential right to marry his cousin. It is a right of first refusal, but some castes consider it improper for him to refuse, and go so far as to outcaste parents who marry a daughter to some one else without giving their nephew the option of marrying her. In some castes, again, a man has a preferential right to marry his sister's daughter. Under this system of cousin marriages the bridegroom is sometimes quite young, while his wife is of mature age, possibly old enough to be his mother. In such a contingency his father or his father's brother may beget children for him, but the boy is their putative father. The castes which allow this practice have the grace to be ashamed of it, and it will probably fall in time into desuetude.

Marriages of this kind are believed to have been due to the desire of fathers under the matrilineal system to arrange marriages so that their property, which would otherwise pass to their sister's sons, should be inherited by their own sons. They retain their hold on the people not only because of the reverence attached to custom, but also because of their practical convenience, for they curtail the expenses of a marriage, they avoid the necessity for payments to the bridegroom's family, and they prevent the dispersion of family property, and on the latter account, unorthodox though they are, they have even found their way into Brahman circles.[1]

Exogamy is the prevailing rule among the tribes as distinct from castes, i.e. marriages take place outside the clan or sept but within the tribe. It is also found in some castes, a man marrying a girl of another sub-caste and not one of his own; such castes are chiefly castes of a tribal type and castes consisting of Hinduized aboriginals, which practised exogamy before they adopted Hinduism and the caste system. Hypergamy is a modified form of exogamy, for it means that a girl must marry into another group, which must not be of lower social status than her own but must be of equal or preferably higher status. This rule is not infrequently enforced by punishing parents who marry a daughter to a man of a lower group by degrading them to that group. Hypergamy is practised by the higher sections of Brahmans in Bengal and North Bihar, by the Rajputs and some other castes in North India, and by some castes in Malabar. It is also a device employed by sub-castes which are rising in the scale in order to mark their superiority to other sub-castes of the same caste. It is, for instance, common for sub-castes which prohibit the remarriage of widows to refuse to give their girls in marriage to sub-castes which still allow women to marry a second time.

Hypergamy has in the past been a source of abuse owing to the difficulty of getting husbands for girls of the highest groups. The girls being many, and the eligible husbands few, the law

[1] L. K. Anantha Krishna Iyar, *Lectures on Ethnography* (Calcutta, 1925), p. 130.

of supply and demand came into operation and competitive prices were charged for husbands. The Rajputs and others in Rajputana and North-West India found the cost of marrying daughters prohibitive and, to avoid dishonour, killed them at birth. In many a village there was not a single girl to be seen. The Kulin Brahmans were more ingenious and paid complaisant bridegrooms large fees for marrying their girls before puberty. A plurality of wives, such as even Mormonism does not contemplate, was often the result: men are known to have had so many that they had to keep a register of them to refresh their memories. This practice is dying out in Bengal, where it is now very exceptional for a Kulin Brahman to have more than one wife. The difficulty of marrying girls persists, but results in their being married comparatively late. The practice, however, lingers among the Maithil Brahmans of North Bihar, where there is a class of men who sell themselves or their minor sons in marriage to girls of a lower group: some have as many as forty or fifty wives, who live with their parents and are occasionally visited by their husbands.

Even after all the rules as to sub-caste, kinship, &c., have been complied with, the choice of a husband or of a wife is still far from free. The question of ages has to be taken into account, for the bridegroom should be older than the bride. Illiterate castes who do not know the ages of children go by their heights and are satisfied if the boy is two or three inches higher than the girl. The choice is further complicated by astrology, for the horoscopes of both the prospective bride and bridegroom have to be compared, to see whether they agree, whether the union will be a long and happy one, blessed with children, &c. Should it be found that the girl will die before the man, all is well, but should she be destined to outlive him, the match will be called off in order to save her from widowhood with all its unhappiness. The process of elimination by horoscopes is often extraordinarily long. Pandita Ramabai mentions a case in which 300 horoscopes were examined before a suitable bridegroom could be discovered for a girl.[1]

Although a Hindu marriage is a sacrament, the agreements between parents which precede it are of the nature of contracts, without any idea of free choice by the parties or any romantic associations. There is a class of go-betweens, called Ghataks or marriage-brokers in North India, and definite agreements are made as to the sums to be paid to the parents of the bride or bridegroom as the case may be. These payments are made as consideration for the father's consent to the marriage and are known as the bride price and bridegroom price. The former is usual in the lower castes, where brides are in demand, the latter in the higher castes, where there is competition for bridegrooms. The amounts vary according to the wealth and position of the parties and also according to circumstances. For instance, when a bridegroom price is paid, the girl's parents will have to pay more if she has already attained puberty; when a bride price is paid, they will receive less. One thing which affects the price is the lightness or darkness of a girl's complexion. The fairer she is, the more is she in demand and the price of a bridegroom is reduced accordingly, while it goes up if she has the misfortune to be dark and swarthy. 'I am black but comely' is not an Indian sentiment.

A modern innovation is the payment of large sums on account of the educational qualifications of a bridegroom, not so much because they are an asset *per se* as because they are regarded as proof that he will be able to obtain a competence or possibly make a fortune. Boys who have passed the entrance examination of a university command fair prices, B.A.s even more. In the Indian Legislative Assembly in 1924 a Bengali member declared that if a bridegroom was a B.A., Rs. 5,000 might be demanded by his parents, while the price went higher for a M.A. Another Bengali member capped this by

[1] *The High-Caste Woman* (Philadelphia, 1887), p. 36.

saying he personally knew of a case in which a bridegroom had actually been sold by auction for Rs. 19,000. In some parts of the Punjab and Sind the system of bride prices among the lower classes has led to a curious form of crime. A bridegroom, or his family, obtains a bride through brokers; and owing to local shortage of women, girls are imported for the purpose from distant places. Frauds are perpetrated, women of low caste being palmed off on men of higher caste, and sometimes women are kidnapped and actually sold.

No question of a bride price arises where a young man wins his bride by service, as is the case among some aboriginal tribes and some of the lowest castes. The young man is usually one who is too poor to pay for a bride. He therefore works in the house of her parents for some years, after which she is given to him as his wife, in the same way that Leah and Rachel were given to Jacob.

It is one of the many inequalities of the sexes that while a woman may, according to orthodox Hindu belief, marry only once, a man is bound by no such rule. He may marry again if he is a widower, and he may even marry a second wife during the lifetime of his first, if she suffers from an incurable disease or has not given birth to a son; the need of a son is so urgent that a second wife is sometimes taken with the consent, and even at the request, of the first wife. The rule, as laid down by the Laws of Manu, is that a wife who is barren may be superseded by another in the eighth year after marriage, one whose children have all died in the tenth year, and one who is unfortunate enough to have only daughters, in the eleventh year; a virago may be superseded without delay. There is also no objection to a man marrying for a second or a third or even a fourth time, if, and when, he becomes a widower. A third marriage being unlucky, he will be well advised if he formally marries a tree, so that his next marriage to a woman will be his fourth, on which he may enter without fear of the consequences. A case is known of a childless Maharaja whose first two wives died soon after marriage. He was next married to a tree, and his fourth marriage was blessed by a son. There is often great disparity of age, elderly widowers commonly marrying quite young girls not only because of their personal preferences, but also because of the belief of parents in the necessity of early marriage for their daughters.

The marriage of widows is not only permissible but quite common in the Moslem community. In orthodox Hindu circles, however, marriage is regarded as indissoluble either by divorce or by the death of the husband. The remarriage of a widow is accordingly looked upon with abhorrence, even if she is a virgin widow whose husband died when she was a child. Remarriage of widows is legally possible under an Act passed in 1856 which, however, while permitting it, deprives a widow of any property inherited by her from her husband— a provision which may appear harsh to a European but is eminently reasonable in the opinion of Hindus because on remarriage she passes into her new husband's family. Advantage is rarely taken of the Act by members of the higher castes, as remarriage is contrary to scriptural authority as well as tradition and custom. The traditional view is simply that as a woman can only be born once and die once, she can only be married once, and that a widow should lead a life of self-denial and renunciation. According to the Laws of Manu, 'When her lord is deceased she should not even pronounce the name of another man, and should cheerfully practise the incomparable rules of virtue which have been followed by such women as were devoted to one only husband.' Her reward is the attainment of heaven; 'a virtuous wife', says the same authority, 'ascends to heaven, though she have no child, if after the decease of her lord she devote herself to pious austerity'.

The miseries of the lot of a high-caste widow have often

been depicted. She renounces the world as surely as a nun taking the veil—and it must not be forgotten that renunciation is in consonance with Hindu ideals—her hair (a woman's glory in the view of Hindus as well as early Christians) is cut off; she can only wear plain clothes with no ornaments; she cannot attend family festivities as she is a woman of ill omen; she has a meal only once a day (though it is more substantial than that of a married woman); she must go without food and even drink twice a month. To add to her misery, the death of her husband is ascribed to sins committed by her in a previous life. If she is a child-widow, her lot is not so unhappy, as she continues to live in her father's house, but she is doomed to lifelong celibacy. She has no opportunity of giving way to natural instincts and will never know the joys of motherhood, unless, as unfortunately sometimes happens, she falls from the paths of virtue, in which case she will be outcasted and her children will be a curse instead of a blessing. If her husband's death occurs after she has become a wife in fact as well as in name, her lot depends on whether she has children and particularly sons, for a widow with sons is held in high honour. If, however, she is childless, her husband's family is apt to regard her as an incubus, and she often drags through a dreary life condemned to lifelong domestic service as a maid-of-all-work.

Much, however, depends on the personal equation. Not all relations-in-law are either heartless or unkind, and it has been pointed out before now that the common stories of the general ill-treatment of widows are either exaggerated or too sweeping. The Rev. Bihari Lal Day wrote in *Bengal Peasant Life*:

'The idea that a Hindu widow is persecuted and tormented by her relations and friends is a fiction of foreign writers, of people unacquainted with Hindu life in its actual manifestations. There are, no doubt, exceptional cases, but as a general rule Hindu widows are not only not ill-treated, but they meet with a vast deal of sympathy. Old widows in a Bengali Hindu family are often the guides and counsellors of those who style themselves the lords of creation.'

Mr. M. C. Mullick goes farther and remarks in *A Study in Ideals: Great Britain and India*: 'In respectable families widowed daughters and sisters are the pets of the household and receive more kind treatment than daughters-in-law, who, being strangers from another family, are regarded with suspicion until they become mothers.' Recently again Mrs. Sarangadhar Das has pointed out that in innumerable houses, a widow, instead of being persecuted, is cherished. Those around her do their best to alleviate the hardships of her life, while she herself is the untiring nurse of the sick and leads a life of self-service to others.[1] Still, when all has been said, the widow's life is generally a pathetic one and also a long one, the result presumably of her simple and abstemious life. A common expression on the lips of an aged widow in Bengal is, 'Shall I never die? Yama (the god of death) seems to have forgotten me'—a fact which speaks for itself.[2]

The traditional view about the marriage of widows is being given up by the more advanced and better-educated members of the Hindu community. The Arya Samaj has set itself against the prohibition of widow remarriage, and societies have been started which seek to encourage it and so remove the social opprobrium attaching to it: one of the most successful has been founded in the Punjab, where its work is facilitated by the shortage of women and the traffic in imported brides, to which reference has already been made. Needless to say, others oppose the movement, not only for religious but also for economic reasons, on the ground that the competition of widows may render the task of marrying daughters still more difficult.

The remarriage of widows appears never to have been

[1] F. Hauswirth, *Purdah* (1932), p. 79.
[2] S. C. Bose, *The Hindoos as they are* (1881), pp. 238, 253.

prohibited by the lower castes, whose social customs in this, as in many other respects, do not conform to Brahmanical rules. It is quite a common custom in some parts: indeed, Mr. Crooke, writing about the United Provinces, says 'as a matter of fact among all but the very high castes every young widow finds another mate'.[1] But Brahmanical influence is so strong that marriage to a widow is looked upon with little favour even by those which allow it. It is attended by scarcely any of the rites customary to a marriage. Some celebrate such a marriage only at night; others allow none but widowers to marry widows, though this rule may be got round by an unmarried man first going through a form of marriage to a tree which he cuts down, so as to convert himself symbolically into a widower. Even when remarriage is admissible, many of the castes show their disapproval of it by treating both the woman and her husband with contempt, so much so that the woman is looked upon as little better than a concubine. It is understandable, therefore, that there is a general tendency to give up widow remarriage as being a disreputable practice. Its abandonment raises a caste or sub-caste in social esteem, and those which discountenance it either rank higher or have at least greater prestige than those which permit it.

One form of widow remarriage which is in vogue among the Jats and some Hindu castes, as well as among aboriginal tribes, is at first sight like the levirate of the Jews by which a man raised up seed to his brother. Under this custom a widow in India is married to her deceased husband's brother, but there the resemblance ends. There is no idea that the line of the dead brother should be continued; on the contrary, a widow who already has children may be married to her brother-in-law just as much as a childless widow, and children of the second marriage belong to the actual father. The idea is rather that the widow is a valuable piece of property, for whom

[1] *The North-Western Provinces of India* (1897), p. 229.

a bride price has been paid, and should not be allowed to go out of the family.

The second husband in this form of widow remarriage must be a younger brother of the deceased, and among some castes and tribes neither party is obliged to marry, though it is regarded as the proper thing for them to do and pressure may be put on a reluctant widow to win her consent. Sir George Campbell states that, when he was a young Magistrate in the cis-Sutlej States, he found that Jat widows were by established custom under an obligation to marry their deceased husband's brothers. The men insisted that they should discharge it, but the women had a contrary way of asserting their independence by refusing to do so. Many a dispute of this kind was referred to the young Magistrate, whose rule was simply that the women should show reasonable cause for their refusal.

'If', wrote this upholder of tribal law, 'the man seemed a decent man, and the woman could give no better reason than to say "I don't like him", I said "Stuff and nonsense! I can't listen to that. The law must be respected"; and I sometimes married them then and there by throwing a sheet over them after the native fashion for second marriage. So far as I could learn those marriages generally turned out very happily.'[1]

Another exception to the general rule that marriage for a Hindu woman is single and indissoluble is found in Malabar among castes other than the Brahman. There are two stages in a marriage in that part of the country. The first ceremony, which serves as a prologue to marriage, is known as tying on the *tali*, i.e. a string, on which a small piece of gold is threaded, is tied round the girl's neck. This rite is looked on as a wedding and must be performed before puberty: otherwise a girl may be outcasted. Cohabitation with the bridegroom after the ceremony is the exception rather than the rule, and the man very often has no more to do with the girl. It merely gives her

[1] *Memoirs of my Indian Career* (1893), vol. i, pp. 82–3.

MARRIAGE

a marriageable status and makes her competent to go on to the second stage. To avoid the incidental expenses of a series of weddings, each with a separate feast, it is a common practice for all the girls in a family (sometimes including even infants) to go through the rite simultaneously—a kind of mass marriage.

The second stage is called *sambandham*, or presenting a cloth, as it is celebrated by the bridegroom giving a bridal cloth to the bride. This is more properly a marriage, for it is celebrated when the girl has attained years of discretion, and it is followed by cohabitation. In a way it resembles companionate marriage, for its continuance depends on the consent of both parties. Either may terminate it at any time by a deed of separation, and there is no bar, either social or religious, to remarriage. In practice, however, unions of this kind are very often permanent, ending only with death, and the wives, while free to leave their husbands and to enter into fresh marriage relations, are said to be chaste and faithful.

This kind of marriage is closely connected with the matriarchal system found on the Malabar coast. The wife does not become a member of her husband's family: the children belong to her family, not his; he is under no obligation to maintain either her or them. It is in favour with the younger sons of Nambudri Brahman families, who are precluded from regular marriages with women of their own caste, that being a privilege reserved to the eldest brother. They therefore enter into *sambandham* marriages with Nair and other women, an arrangement which has the advantage of relieving the ancestral property from the expense of supporting their wives and families.

The Malabar Marriage Act passed in 1896 provides that, if a *sambandham* marriage is regularly registered, the wife and children are entitled to be maintained by the man and to succeed to half his self-acquired property, besides which the parties cannot contract a second *sambandham* marriage unless the first is terminated by death or a formal application for divorce in

the Civil Courts. Very little use has been made of these provisions, both because men do not like to submit to restrictions
on their liberty to contract second marriages, and also because
by another Act passed two years later husbands can provide
for their wives and children without registration.

Divorce in India is a man's privilege. Among Hindus it is
confined to the lower castes, whose husbands put away their
wives on account of infidelity and sometimes also barrenness
or incurable disease—a practice sanctioned by customary law
but not recognized by sacred law.[1] There are no formal proceedings, and repudiation is symbolized by removing the
insignia of a married woman, such as the iron bangle round her
wrist, or by tearing some leaves of a tree. Women have no
right, however, to dissolve the marriage tie, save in such
exceptional cases as the Malabar marriages mentioned above.
Divorce is almost equally one-sided under Moslem law. It is
open to a husband to divorce his wife not only for a definite
reason such as misconduct but also without assigning any
reason whatever. It is, moreover, possible for a man to divorce
his wife by repeating three times a formula of repudiation[2]
(*talaq*), and this makes divorce simple and easy. A husband
has merely to pronounce the fatal words of repudiation thrice
before two witnesses and his separation from his wife is final
and irrevocable. The threefold repetition was no doubt
intended to give a husband time for reflection as to the

[1] In the State of Baroda a Divorce Act was passed (for Hindus) in 1931,
which allows divorce on a number of grounds and gives wives as well as
husbands the right of divorce. The grounds are adultery, a husband's
impotence, pregnancy without the husband's knowledge, bigamy on the
part of a wife, disappearance for 7 years, becoming a recluse, conversion
to another religion, cruelty, desertion without reasonable cause, and
addiction to intoxicants to the prejudice of the fulfilment of marital
obligations.

[2] This is perhaps the commonest form of divorce, though it is least
approved of by respectable Moslems. There are other forms of repudiation which are not at once irrevocable.

consequences of his action, to make him realize that divorce is not a thing to be undertaken lightly or unadvisedly; but unfortunately he can repeat the formula without an interval. If he does so in a temporary fit of temper in the presence of two other persons, his wife is *ipso facto* divorced, and even if he repents, he is unable to remarry her; though this difficulty may be got round by means of a legal fraud, for if she is again married and again divorced, he may again make her his wife. She can therefore be formally married to, and immediately divorced by, another man, after which she and her first husband can remarry. As a matter of fact a Moslem is often deterred from proceeding to the third and final repetition of the words by knowledge of the consequences and, in particular, the law as to 'dower'. 'Dower' is a settlement on the wife, made by the prenuptial contract, out of her husband's property, and may be (either in whole or in part) 'prompt', i.e. made over to her at the time of marriage, or 'deferred', i.e. payable on the dissolution of her marriage either by death or divorce. The knowledge that a deferred dower can be claimed is calculated to make a husband hesitate before he makes a divorce irrevocable and to serve, therefore, as some protection for a wife. Even if no specified amount is fixed by contract, the wife is entitled to 'proper' dower, i.e. the sum which is usually provided for other women of her family who have already been married. The amounts settled on the wife in this way are sometimes very large, as it is regarded as a point of honour by well-born but needy Moslems to contract to pay large sums, which are out of all proportion to their means: a man earning £5 a month may, for instance, name a sum equal to £5,000 as the dower to be settled on his wife. Where there is a contract for dower, a Court must award the full amount agreed upon unless there is a statutory enactment, as in Oudh and Ajmer-Merwara, by which it has power to reduce the amount to a sum proportionate to the husband's means. But, whatever may be the decree of the Court, its execution depends on the man's ability to pay. You cannot get blood out of a stone, and this the husband knows perfectly well. Although, therefore, there may be an idea that a husband who is under contract to pay a huge sum will think twice before divorcing his wife and making himself at once liable, the check is more imaginary than real. In practice the husband's power of divorce is almost unlimited and it is frequently abused; in Eastern Bengal husbands are said to cast off their wives as easily as their old clothes.[1]

A Moslem wife can obtain a divorce in one of three ways. She and her husband may agree, either before or after marriage, that in certain circumstances approved by Islamic law she will have the power of repudiation just as the husband has. Under this arrangement she can act, and act quite effectively, under a power which is really delegated to her by her husband. A second form of divorce, called *khula*, is effected at the instance of a wife when she has given or agreed to give consideration to her husband for her release from the marriage tie; his consent is essential. A third form is that called *mubarak*, which is divorce by mutual consent of husband and wife, and which operates as a complete discharge of marital rights on either side.

Very few Hindu husbands have more than one wife. Polygamy is practised by some primitive tribes, which regard a plurality of wives as a sign of wealth, and also by some cultivating castes in the Central Provinces, which find that it pays to have one wife for housework and another for field work. Otherwise it is confined to the exceptional cases already mentioned, viz. those in which a man's first wife is childless and those rare cases in which it is due to hypergamy among a few Brahman sub-castes, and in which it may be a mere form. Moslems are also generally monogamous, though polygamy is permissible on the authority of a text in the Koran, which

[1] S. Khuda Baksh, *Essays: Indian and Islamic* (1912), p. 258.

says that a man may marry two or three or four wives, and that if he cannot deal equally with all, he may marry only one. Some hold that this permission being conditional on equality of treatment, and the latter being humanly impossible, it is in essence an injunction against polygamy, but the general view and practice are to the contrary. It is recognized that the practice helps to provide homes for women, especially widows, who might otherwise be destitute, but it is generally felt that though lawful, it is not expedient. Most Moslems are too poor to be able to afford more than one wife. Even those who can afford a plurality of wives object to it both on moral grounds and on the common-sense ground that the polygamist's life is not a happy one. A polygamous house is one divided against itself, and the unfortunate man who has two wives or more has little peace or happiness; according to a proverb current in North India, two cats and one mouse, two wives in one house, two dogs with one bone, cannot get on together. The system is, in fact, as remarked by an accomplished Moslem writer, a fruitful source of discord, strife, and harassing litigation—the ruin of many wealthy families.[1]

Polyandry is so rare a phenomenon as to be negligible in a consideration of the social system of India. It is confined to some of the Himalayan races and a few communities in the interior. Among the former may be mentioned the Ladakhis, the Bhotias of Sikkim, whose forefathers brought the custom with them from the Tibetan plateau, the Kanets, and some other low castes of Kulu and other parts of the Punjab Hills; among the latter are the Santals of the Santal Parganas and Chota Nagpur, the Todas of the Nilgiri Hills, and a few low castes in Malabar and Travancore. Maternal polyandry, under which there is a plurality of husbands who need not be related *inter se*, and who are not responsible for the maintenance of the woman or her children, is exceptional but is found

[1] S. Khuda Baksh, *Essays: Indian and Islamic* (1912), p. 257.

among the Muduvars of Travancore, where it is subject to the rule that the husbands must not be brothers or cousins on the paternal side.

The prevalent type is fraternal polyandry, i.e. a woman who marries a man also becomes the common wife of his brothers. The paternity of the children is settled in different ways. They may be regarded as the common children of all the brothers, or of the eldest brother only, in which case his brothers are called uncles; or the eldest brother is treated as the father of the first child, the next eldest of the second child, and so on; or the mother nominates one of the brother-husbands as the father of any particular child. Fraternal polyandry is accompanied among the Santals by a strange form of sororal polygamy. Polyandry is so far practised that the wife of an eldest brother has marital relations with his younger brothers until they are married. The practice is limited by the personal equation, for not all men are ready to allow their younger brothers access to their wives nor do wives themselves always acquiesce in this arrangement. At the same time, a wife's younger sisters have conjugal relations with her husband so long as they are unmarried; and though Santal wives are as a rule frantically jealous, they not only tolerate their sisters sharing their husbands, but even encourage them. Polyandry and polygamy also co-exist among the Todas, among whom, for example, two brothers may have two wives in common.

VIII

THE PURDAH SYSTEM

THE purdah[1] system is a term descriptive of the custom by which many women in India live in seclusion at home and, if they go out, are screened from public view by such devices as veiling the face, or covering the whole person, or hanging curtains over the windows of railway and other carriages, motor-cars, and palanquins. The system is confined to a minority of the population, and in some parts of the country is almost unknown. It is general among the more well-to-do Moslems throughout India and among the higher Hindu castes in North India, but even there it has not been adopted by the lower castes. In South India it does not obtain among the Hindus with the exception of the Nambudri Brahmans of Malabar, and it is not observed by Moplahs and is less rigid among other Moslems than among their co-religionists in the north. It is not practised by the Marathas in West India, whose women appear freely in public, and it is absent from a large part of Gujarat. It is also not practised by any of the Mongolian tribes on the frontier or of the aboriginal tribes of the interior.

In view of the misapprehension which exists as to the extent of the purdah system, it cannot be too strongly emphasized that the great majority of the women of India lead a perfectly natural life, though there is not full and free association with

[1] Purdah (*parda*) means a curtain, and the word *parda-nishin*, i.e. one who sits behind a curtain, and inferentially is not seen, is used of women who live in seclusion. They are sometimes called *gosha*, which is an English contraction of *gosha-nishin*, i.e. one who sits in a corner. The word zenana, which means women, but is applied to the rooms in which they live, is also used in this connexion but not altogether aptly, for though the houses of people of any position have special women's quarters, the women who live in them are not necessarily secluded.

the opposite sex as in the west: a woman who is familiar with men is thought immodest, if not immoral. Like women in other countries, besides doing domestic work, they go to market, visit their friends, and mix with their neighbours, particularly at the village well or on the bank of the river or reservoir from which they fetch water, and at which they bathe and gossip. Large numbers assist their husbands in agricultural and industrial work and are saleswomen for the products of their labour. It is a common thing for women to take to market such things as the pots made on the potter's wheel, the fish caught in the rivers, the wood cut down in the forests, or—the common substitute for wood in disforested tracts—the cakes which they themselves make from cow-dung, straw, and litter. Large numbers, moreover, are working women. They are chiefly engaged in cottage industries, but there are some 350,000 employed in factories and other industrial concerns, and 50,000 in mines (chiefly as loaders), and it has already been found necessary in some provinces to start factory welfare work, crèches for children, &c., and to pass Maternity Benefits Acts.

There is no religious sanction for the purdah system, either Islamic or Hindu; it is merely a custom established for many centuries. The Moslems appear first to have adopted it in imitation of the Persians during the eighth century, when the licentiousness of Walid II forced them to segregate their women as a safeguard against attacks on their chastity.[1] The practice of absolute seclusion and segregation does not appear to have become general among them till the end of the tenth century. It was introduced by them into India and was adopted by the Hindus, with whom purdah had hitherto been the rare privilege of princesses and ladies of high rank. Their adoption of it was partly due to the influence of the courts on noblemen and officials, who followed the example of their

[1] Syed Ameer Ali, *Short History of the Saracens* (1916), pp. 199, 455.

Moslem masters, partly to the desire to protect their women-kind and not to expose them either to risk or temptation. No race is more sensitive about the chastity of its women, and seclusion seemed the best means of safeguarding it. The practice once introduced became sanctified by custom, and custom is still its basis.

It varies in intensity in different localities and in different communities. It is most strictly observed by Moslems of the upper classes, some of whom will relegate girls to the seclusion of the house as early as the age of four; generally the earliest age at which close seclusion begins is eight or nine and the latest twelve, by which time girls in India have generally attained puberty. The farther one goes north-west, where Moslems predominate, the more does the practice prevail. It is in the north-west that the *burkah* is found: this is a kind of shroud with eye-holes, which envelops the whole person from head to foot. Elsewhere women are usually content to cover their heads with the cloths which drape their persons. There is a great difference between practice in towns and villages. In the villages women have much more liberty, especially in places like Bengal, where the people live in detached homesteads, each with a pond or tank from which water can be drawn and with clumps of bamboos round it which afford an effectual screen. Segregation is much more complete and the conditions of life more unhealthy in towns and cities with houses closely packed together. There purdah can only be kept up by adjusting domestic architecture to the need of securing privacy for the ladies of the household. They live in the inner apartments, where they will be safe from intrusion, and, to add to their security, the windows are placed high up in the walls, are closely latticed, and are few in number and small in size, so that the rooms get insufficient light and ventilation.

Among Hindus two communities which keep their women

in the strictest segregation and seclusion are the Nambudri Brahmans of Malabar and the Rajputs of Rajputana and the Kangra Hills in the Punjab. The name given to Nambudri women is eloquent: it means those who stay inside, or the indoors people. They must not look on the face of, or be seen by, any males except their husbands, and they rarely go outside their houses. If they go for a walk, they are screened from sight by a large palmyra-leaf umbrella, which is called the 'mask umbrella'. If they are forced to travel, they go in a palanquin which is preceded by a Nair woman, who acts as a crier, warning away all males by a long-drawn-out shout. The 'mask umbrella' is regarded as a symbol of chastity, and is taken away from any woman who is excommunicated for misconduct.[1]

Purdah is a cherished institution of the Rajputs, to which they cling in spite of the inconvenience it causes; because of it the men in some places have to do women's work like drawing water and chopping wood. It is maintained with special rigour by the Rajputs of the Kangra Hills who build their houses, if possible, near a wood which will serve as a protective screen. If this cannot be arranged, privacy is ensured by a vestibule some fifty yards from the house, beyond which no stranger may pass. Should they be forced to travel, their women are conveyed in palanquins screened from view; if they are unable to afford this conveyance, they travel by night along unfrequented paths. The women themselves are passionately attached to purdah and shrink from appearing in public because it would mean a sacrifice of honour. A case is known in which a house caught fire in the day-time, and there being no neighbouring wood in which they could take shelter, the women elected to stay in the house and be burnt to death rather than expose themselves to the public gaze.[2]

[1] W. Logan, *Malabar* (Madras, 1887), pp. 125, 127.
[2] *Kangra Hills District Gazetteer* (Lahore, 1926), p. 164.

There was a similar system in ancient Greece, the description of which by Lecky in the *History of European Morals* would apply in a large measure to the purdah system of India. The wives of the Greeks were usually married very young and they were under tutelage first to their parents, who disposed of their hands, and then to their husbands, fidelity to whom was their first duty. They lived in a special retired part of the house,[1] where they were engaged in domestic occupations, such as weaving, spinning, embroidery, and household management. 'The prevailing manners were very gentle'—words which are fairly applicable to the high-caste women of India. They enjoyed remarkable freedom from temptation, and were protected by public opinion, which was dead against any attempts at seduction. Custom rendered their purely domestic life a second nature, but their minds must necessarily have been exceedingly contracted by its narrowness and by the absence of the educating influence of male society.

These features are as characteristic of the Indian purdah system as they were of the Greek system. Purdah has proved an effectual safeguard to virtue; it may be a fugitive and cloistered virtue, but virtue all the same. On the other hand, it must be laid to its charge that it keeps a woman in a narrow circle and prevents full mental development. A girl's education generally ends when she goes into purdah, though it may be continued if her parents are alive to the value of education, and if arrangements can be made for private tuition or for sending her to a girls' school in a covered carriage or bus. She is not left without training, but it is of a special kind, being

---

[1] Cornelius Nepos wrote that Greek women were not admitted to any feasts except those of relatives, and lived in an inner part of the house (called *gynaekonitis*, i.e. the women's quarters), which no one entered unless they were close relatives. He contrasted the liberty allowed to Roman women with that denied to women in Greece; but it is worth pointing out that the Romans regarded as the ideal wife Bona Dea, whose face, while she was on earth, was seen by no man but her husband.

almost entirely a training in domestic matters. When she leaves her own home for her husband's she has to undergo a pretty strict discipline, the first lesson in which is subordination, not only to her husband, but also to her mother-in-law and to the grandmother-in-law, who lay down the law in social and domestic matters. She is taught that her life must be one of subjection to authority and of service to her husband and his family. She is so much cut off from male society that she may neither speak to her husband's father and elder brother nor even speak in their presence unless asked to do so. In Northern India she should even cover her face when they come into the room— a kind of purdah within purdah.

The purdah woman's horizon is bounded by the four walls of the house; her duties are mainly domestic and religious, for the observance of household rites is part and parcel of Hindu family life. In an educated household the régime is different and intellectual interests are given scope, but generally speaking the life of a purdah woman is far from intellectual. There is a prejudice against modern education in conservative Hindu houses, and a fear that a girl may lose the traditional virtues of a Hindu if she is educated on modern lines. In old-fashioned circles contempt is felt for both European women and educated Indian women, who, it is believed, become Europeanized. It is thought that they neglect their work and read novels all day, neither respect their husbands nor nurse their babies, and are generally immodest and unwomanly.[1]

Defective as it undoubtedly is from an educational point of view, the purdah system has a value of its own in the formation of character. There is a general consensus among those who know purdah women as to the charming type which purdah produces, at any rate among the upper classes. Lady Dufferin remarked that she had never seen women more sympathetic, more full of grace and dignity, or more courteous, and Mrs.

[1] See G. S. Dutt, *A Woman of India* (1929), pp. 83, 106.

Urquhart says that the well-bred Hindu girl is distinguished by remarkable sweetness and charm of manner, perfect politeness, and a quaint motherly bearing, and is a model for all the world to follow as regards politeness to elder persons and the care of infants.[1] If I may speak from a small acquaintance with ladies who have come out of purdah, I may confirm these accounts; for the impression I received was one of quiet dignity and refinement, gentleness and grace, so much so that I could not help thinking that if ladies such as these were typical products of the purdah system, at any rate in families of good birth and means, there must be something to be said for it. 'Do men gather grapes of thorns, or figs of thistles?'

Nor is the system incompatible with the development of stronger qualities such as power of conduct and capacity for management. When the young girl in course of time becomes the head of the family, she shows her capability in social and domestic matters. Many purdah women exercise an influence not only on social, but also on political life which is at first sight surprising considering their seclusion; it is well known that the nationalist movement has found support in, and even inspiration from, the zenana. Many purdah women show remarkable shrewdness and judgement in estate management, and cases are known in which they have proved strong and capable rulers of Indian States.

It is impossible, however, to deny that in the majority of cases purdah life is unhealthy, both physically and mentally. Anaemia, osteomalacia, and tuberculosis are all too common consequences of life within the walls of a house and want of fresh air and exercise; only too often purdah women lead an idle objectless life, with interests confined to dress, jewellery, gossip, and petty intrigue. On the whole, it may be said that they are intellectually backward and have a narrow outlook on life. Nothing else can be expected when they are cut

[1] See W. E. S. Holland, *The Goal of India* (1928), p. 99.

off from intercourse with the outside world and have little association with men even in their homes. It is on this account that educated young men show an increasing disinclination to marry young purdah girls who are unable to give them intellectual companionship. This appears to be a modern development of education on western lines. So far as can be seen, there used formerly to be no such gulf between the sexes when the education both of boys and girls followed traditional Indian lines. Now, however, the gulf exists, and it is widening; the interests of men who have received an English education have broadened, those of women remain restricted. The view expressed by the Raja of Nabha to Sir Walter Lawrence is shared by many thoughtful men. 'We educate our sons, teach them English and western ideas, and then marry them to girls who have had no education. The result will be a breed of mules.'[1]

It is also obviously against the economic interests of the country that a large part of its womankind should be confined to domestic work and that their services cannot be utilized for the general welfare or for active and organized charity. The needs of Indian women, both educational and medical, should be met by Indian women, but in 1930–1 throughout the whole of the country there were only 235 women studying in medical colleges and 186 in training colleges for teachers. In addition to all this, the segregation of many of the best representatives of their sex tends to lower the moral tone of the community. The influence of purdah in this direction cannot be better expressed than in the words of a Bengali lady, Saroj Nalini (Mrs. G. S. Dutt), who devoted her life to the social advancement of her countrywomen.

'It is because our good women are kept secluded that the level of morality among our men in public as well as in private life has sunk so low. A people who keep their chaste women carefully hidden behind high walls and heavy veils shut out their influence

[1] Sir Walter Lawrence, *The India we served* (1928), p. 111.

from social and national life. Among such a people men are bound to go wrong.'[1]

It is generally agreed that purdah could not endure but would be set aside if only the purdah women themselves would make a common stand against it, but at present they are its staunchest supporters. They are not merely content with but proud of their lot. They are as much attached to purdah as devout nuns to the conventual life, but from different motives. They do not regard purdah as a refuge from the world and a shield against its perils, but as an outward and visible sign of virtue and chastity, as well as a patent of respectability. In their eyes, giving up purdah would mean going down in the world and reducing themselves to the level of the lower classes. Their feelings are backed by their strong conservatism, and a man who wishes the women of his family to come out of purdah, either because he entertains enlightened views or because its expense is more than he can afford, has to overcome determined opposition on their part. Their view that purdah stands for chastity is supported by outside opinion, and this adds to the difficulty of women leading an independent life. A woman of the upper classes living without the protection of her family suffers such a loss of reputation that she may even be looked upon as a fallen woman. Ladies who go out into the world and take up independent work as doctors or schoolmistresses only too often find that they are regarded as fair game by vicious young men of their own rank in life. Knowledge of this naturally affects the standpoint of purdah women themselves when the question of abandoning purdah is raised.

Unfortunately too, purdah being a custom most prevalent among the upper classes, the lower classes associate it with social superiority and try to follow their example. Purdah, so to speak, is fashionable, and the lower classes in India, as else-

[1] G. S. Dutt, *A Woman of India* (1929), p. 74.

where, like to be in the fashion. Families whose women have led a free and open-air life will therefore seclude them as soon as they can afford to do so; a larger income is required to make up for the loss of their labour and to meet the expense of a separate establishment and separate servants for them. The system consequently spreads downwards to new circles, and it may also extend to communities or localities where it was formerly unknown; it is said to have been introduced among the people of Kathiawar only within the last fifty years.

On the other hand, there is a movement among the educated classes in favour of the abolition of purdah, which grows stronger as time goes on and enlightened ideas spread wider. An extraordinary impetus has been given to it by political influences during the last few years, and especially by Mr. Gandhi's appeal to women to take part in the civil disobedience movement. He called on them for help in his campaign against liquor shops and foreign goods, and thousands of Hindu women, inspired both by nationalist fervour and a passion for self-sacrifice in what they regarded as service to their country, responded to his summons, more particularly in Bombay, where they have long been more emancipated than elsewhere. They were enrolled in a body called Desh Sevikas or servants of the country, joined in political processions, attended political meetings, picketed shops, and openly sold *khaddar* (home-spun cloth). Old as well as young rallied to the call, but the majority were of high caste and good education. In Bombay many were university students, to which perhaps may be largely ascribed their political zeal and readiness to defy custom. Their enthusiasm and persistence were almost as strong as those of the suffragettes before the War, and like them they did not hesitate to come into conflict with the police, without, however, the hysterical violence of the suffragette movement in England. In her illuminating book *Purdah*, Mrs. Sarangadhar Das mentions more than one instance of the way in which purdah has been discarded which would have been thought incredible even twenty years ago. In Meerut, for example, 5,000 women came out of purdah as a protest against Mr. Gandhi's arrest and never went back to it. Another instance mentioned by her is equally significant of the revolutionary change which has been effected and is not without an element of humour. A young man who had been educated abroad was anxious to induce the ladies of his household to emancipate themselves, but all his efforts failed to shake their opposition to the change. Once they were carried away on the wave of political fervour, the case was very different. His wife, his mother, and his sisters devoted themselves to the boycott movement. All went to jail at one time or another; the mother, who had hitherto been ultra-conservative, was actually imprisoned thrice. So little were they at home that in the evening after his day's work the young man had to cook his food himself, feed his children, and put them to bed.[1]

[1] F. Hauswirth, *Purdah* (1932), pp. 9, 238.

IX

SOCIAL CHANGES

THE problem of social reform in India is complicated by the close connexion which the social system has with Hinduism. Hinduism does not merely inculcate religious beliefs. It also lays down laws of conduct for social life. Social institutions rest on theological authority; a man's status is believed to be determined by religion, and religious prescriptions largely regulate his manner of life.

'You cannot think', wrote Sir Surendranath Banerjea in 1925, 'of a social question affecting the Hindu community that is not bound up with religious considerations. . . . The social reformer in India has to fight against forces believed to be semi-divine in their character and more or less invulnerable against the common-place and mundane weapons of expediency and common sense.'[1]

The interpreters of religion to the people and the exponents of the religious basis of social customs are the Brahmans, who have always been anxious to maintain the *status quo* or to allow such modifications only as will not impair their authority. Their view of Hinduism is like that of Judaism expressed by Isaac Disraeli, viz. that everything in it is ancient and nothing is obsolete. 'The thing that hath been, it is that which shall be; and that which is done is that which shall be done.' They are never at a loss for a sacred text which can be quoted as a sanction for established custom. Thus, when the question of abolishing suttee was debated, they quoted a verse from the Rig-Veda[2] in support of it, though the lines were garbled and that ancient work gave no sanction to the practice. They were formerly in an almost impregnable position, for the Vedas had

---

[1] *A Nation in making* (1925), p. 396.

[2] An ancient Sanskrit work, in which the Hindus believe as if it were a divine revelation.

Y

been neither printed nor published, but were committed to memory and taught orally. The Brahman was therefore the sole repository of canonical law, and, as Max Müller pointed out, no one could contradict him except those who did not wish to contradict him.[1]

Now that others have the key to the Vedas, the position of the Brahmans as the only arbiters in social, as well as religious, matters has been undermined. An appeal can be, and is, made by Hindu reformers to the picture of pristine society as given in the Vedas, which knew nothing of the present elaborate caste system, and did not recognize child marriages or purdah, but allowed women to lead a free and natural life. Practices of the present day are shown to have no sanction in the most ancient of the Hindu scriptures, and to be not an essential component of Hinduism, but later accretions. They are not without warrant in the scriptures of later date, from which the Brahmans can quote texts to their purpose, but these later writings have not the same authority as the earlier scriptures, which are believed to be of divine inspiration. 'Back to the Vedas' was the slogan of Dayanand Saraswati, the founder of the Arya Samaj, which seeks to restore an earlier and simpler form of Hinduism and, by ridding it of excrescences, to effect both religious and social reform. It advocates monotheism, it denounces idolatry, the evil of child marriages, and the ban on the remarriage of widows, and it favours the abolition of untouchability and reform of the caste system, which, it announces, should rest on the basis of worth, not birth.[2]

A somewhat similar line has been taken in the past by the Government of India, though somewhat tentatively. Lord Lansdowne when Viceroy in 1891, speaking on the Age of Consent Act, said:

[1] *Biographical Essays* (1884), p. 19.

[2] In spite of this no-caste doctrine 94 per cent. of its members made returns of their castes at the census of 1931 in the United Provinces, where the body is strongest.

'In all cases where there is a conflict between the interests of morality and those of religion, the legislature is bound to distinguish, if it can, between essentials and non-essentials, between the great fundamental principles of the religion concerned and the subsidiary beliefs and accretionary dogmas which have accidentally grown up around them. In the case of the Hindu religion such a discrimination is especially needful, and one of the first questions which we have to ask ourselves is, assuming that the practice with which our proposed legislation will interfere is a practice supported by religious sanctions, whether those sanctions are of first-rate importance and absolutely obligatory, or whether they are of minor importance and binding only in a slight degree.'

But it is difficult to know what is essential and what is adventitious. Even if the two can be discriminated by reference to scriptural authority, the popular mind makes no such distinction. This consideration was apparent to Lord William Bentinck when the abolition of suttee was proposed. When it was argued that suttee was not essentially a part of the Hindu religion, he replied that the question was not what the rite was but what it was supposed to be. He had no doubt that the conscientious belief of every order of Hindus with few exceptions regarded it as sacred, but in spite of that, he held that the practice was so inhuman that it must be abolished.

There is a feeling among advanced Indians that social reform should be effected by means of legislation, and complaints are made that Government has been unduly slow to move in this direction. The British Government, being an alien government, has naturally been reluctant to interfere with customs based on religion. With a society so peculiarly constituted as that of the Hindus, religious toleration necessarily involves social toleration, except as regards practices revolting to common humanity like suttee and infanticide. The Government has taken the line that social legislation depends on the consent of the governed and cannot be imposed on an unwilling people. Sir John Malcolm long ago pointed out the danger to British power that would be caused by over-zealous efforts to change the character of the people; and there is the further consideration that legislation in personal matters will be infructuous unless supported by the popular opinion which alone can enforce it, and that the law is brought into contempt if it prescribes impracticable repressions. In addition to this, there is the practical difficulty that the people at large may be absolutely ignorant of the provisions of laws added to the statute book. As recently as 1929, for instance, the Age of Consent Committee reported that the law as to the age of consent was practically unknown throughout the country, knowledge of it being confined to judges, lawyers, and a few educated men. It is perhaps not without significance that when social legislation has been passed for British India, the Indian States, with some exceptions, have until recent years rarely followed suit.

In this connexion, however, legislation permitting a practice must be differentiated from legislation prohibiting one. Thus, the law legalizing the remarriage of widows was merely permissive. It gave legal sanction to a practice which was disapproved of by the higher castes though allowed by the lower; and the number of the former who have taken advantage of its provisions has been infinitesimal, as the feeling against second marriages for widows remains the same. It is a different thing to prohibit an existing practice, which is sanctified by custom, if not by the earliest scriptures: speaking on the latest measure concerning the age of marriage, a member of the Legislative Assembly declared that radical marriage reforms could be effected only if a policeman was put on duty in every orthodox house. Even though suttee was made illegal a little over a century ago, cases of it still occur, though very rarely, and they are approved by a popular sentiment which the law has not been able to eradicate.[1] Even when some poor widow burns herself to death in the privacy of her room by soaking her clothes in kerosene oil and setting them on fire after her husband's death, her act is acclaimed as true to the ideal of Hindu womanhood. An orthodox Hindu who gave evidence before the Joint Select Committee on Indian Constitutional Reforms in August, 1933, caused some surprise by declaring that he approved of the voluntary immolation of widows, which, he said, was considered the highest ideal of humanity. In a subsequent interview he stated: 'The forcible burning of widows was not in accordance with religion and quite rightly was abolished, but when a widow voluntarily dies with her husband, I then regard her as part of divinity.'

The spread of education and of western ideas based on Christian principles has been a more potent instrument of progress than legislation has been or is likely to be. The educated upper classes have examined their old customs and conventions in the light of their new knowledge; but, unlike many of an earlier generation, who often showed a blind admiration of western ways and an unreasoning scorn of their own, the modern generation is more discriminating. They are in favour of keeping all that is good in old customs and of discarding patent abuses, which they recognize to be a reproach to India and not a heritage to be proud of. Increasingly sensitive to outside opinion, they are anxious to do away with practices which

---

[1] Approval is generally merely passive, as when hundreds of gratified spectators came in motor-buses to see a suttee in Patna district. In one extraordinary case, which took place in 1932, it took a violent form. The widow of a Brahman at Fatehpur Sikri declared her intention to burn with the body of her husband but was dissuaded from doing so. Her original intention and subsequent change of mind became known, and a mob collected at her house and demanded that she should undergo suttee. The house was locked against them; but they broke in and dragged the woman off to the burning *ghat* (place of cremation), where they began to erect a funeral pyre. The police, however, appeared on the scene, fired on the mob, and rescued the woman.

may lower India in the estimation of the civilized world; and in this respect the pride of nationalism is a healthy reforming influence. The modern leaders of Indian thought therefore advocate reform, but are not iconoclasts. They recognize that there are many practices which are unhealthy excrescences on Hinduism, the removal of which would make it a sounder and saner social system. They would get rid of irrational usages and make reason, rather than theocratic authority, the standard by which old customs should stand or fall.

The Brahmo Samaj has done much to disseminate ideas of enlightened humanitarianism particularly among the upper classes, and a healthy influence in social matters is exercised by the Arya Samaj. Among others who have laboured for social regeneration may be mentioned the Bengali Brahman, Vidyasagar, to whose efforts was due the Act of 1856 legalizing the remarriage of widows, and the Parsi philanthropist Malabari, who was largely instrumental in securing the enactment of the Age of Consent Act of 1891. Contemporaneous with the latter was Mr. Justice Ranade, a Maratha Brahman, who believed that the crying need of India was social rather than political reform. He was the leader of the Prarthana Samaj, founded in 1867, the objects of which are apparent from the name of its organ, the *Indian Social Reformer*. His wife, Mrs. Ramabai Ranade, at the same time devoted herself to the amelioration of the lot of women and founded the Seva Sadan, a body which has done practical work of a very useful kind among them. With her should be mentioned Pandita Ramabai, the authoress of *The High-Caste Hindu Woman* and the foundress of the Arya Mahila Samaj, a society which aimed at the abolition of child marriage and the raising of the status of women by means of education. A society of a somewhat different type is 'The Servants of India', which was established at Poona by Mr. Gokhale, a disciple of Mr. Justice Ranade and like him a Maratha Brahman. His object was to build up a higher type of character and to train men to devote their lives to the cause of their country in a religious spirit. Every member of the Society takes seven vows, of which one is that his country will always be first in his thoughts and that he will give to her service the best that is in him. Another is that he will regard all Indians as brothers and will work for the advancement of all without distinction of caste or creed. Many of the members renounce the world and devote themselves to a life of social service in fulfilment of their vows.

The working of the spirit of reform is apparent both in the co-operative activities of societies like these and in individual efforts to promote the cause of philanthropy and social service. Both alike are the outcome of a new sense of social duty. The change of outlook on social questions is equally noticeable. A significant symptom is the attitude now adopted towards the vexed question of early marriage compared with forty years ago. When the Age of Consent Bill was introduced in 1890 it roused a storm among the orthodox. Tilak denounced every Hindu who supported it as a renegade and a traitor to his religion. When it was passed in 1891, a popular Bengali newspaper in Calcutta appeared with wild diatribes against the Government and declared that the Hindu religion and Hindu civilization were in danger of destruction. In 1925, however, the age of consent was raised to 13 without any such outbursts, and the Child Marriage Restraint Act of 1929, which is a far more sweeping measure, though denounced as heterodox and irreligious, passed into law in comparative quietude. Whatever may be the effect of the last measure, its peaceful passage is an indication of the extent to which enlightened ideas have spread among the upper classes and their mental outlook has changed.

A distinction must be drawn between the existence of liberal ideas and their translation into practice. Many publicly advocate such reforms as the relaxation of caste restrictions, the breaking of purdah, and the marriage of girls at a later age, but personally shrink from acting up to their precepts for fear of the social consequences. Hinduism allows thought to be free but rigidly controls practice. It combines conservatism in practice with liberalism of belief, in a way which cannot be better explained than by the account of a young Bengali Hindu.

'Even in the most orthodox Indian minds there is a toleration for all shades of thought. It is in the field of practice or observance, especially in the matter of prohibitions, that strictness is demanded and enforced. You may think as you like; but you must not eat the forbidden flesh of cows and pigs; you must not eat food cooked by a man of lower caste; you must not take out your women-folk to mix in male society. . . . Otherwise you come to grief.'[1]

Although, therefore, intellectual belief in Hindu tenets may be lost, its social ordinances continue to be obeyed. There may be an outward compliance with traditional customs and an inward disbelief in them. The attitude is general among the educated classes, and Mrs. Sarangadhar Das goes so far as to say that not more than one out of every ten orthodox Hindus keeps up old customs as a matter of principle and that the others do so through fear of either losing material advantages or social prestige. 'Old customs keep their hold on individuals no longer as principles but from fear of social obloquy. Where fear of detection is removed, many of the most orthodox have no scruple about breaking caste and purdah and often do so with great zest.'[2] It is perhaps on this account that social legislation may be fruitful, as it may strengthen the hands of the weak and enable them to defy convention on the ground that the law must be obeyed and leaves them no option.

The ferment of new ideas, combined with material con-

---

[1] *Report of the Calcutta University Commission* (Calcutta, 1919), vol. i, p. 127.   [2] F. Hauswirth, *Purdah* (1932), pp. 250–1.

siderations, has, however, been sufficient to cause some old taboos to be relaxed or neglected. One instance is that of excommunication for voyages overseas. In some circles no penalty is imposed, in others only a mild penance or ceremony of purification is required. The Hindu community is divided on the subject, the orthodox insisting on keeping up old standards, the modernists giving them up simply because voyages to Europe and elsewhere are necessary for education and profitable employment: for example, the Bhatyas, a trading caste of Gujarat, are divided into two sections, one of which allows and the other absolutely prohibits voyages overseas. In the matter of food and drink there is a similar division, some keeping old scruples, others giving them up and indulging their appetites, except as regards such an utterly obnoxious thing as beef; even a modern sect like the Arya Samaj is divided on the question of diet, one section being eaters of meat and another abjuring it. On the other hand, it should be noticed that low castes tend to give up eating meat under the idea that a vegetarian diet will improve their social status. Even more perhaps have modern influences and economic considerations affected the occupations of the upper classes. They do not scruple to take up trades and professions which they would formerly have scorned, but now find attractive for mercenary reasons, such as boot and shoe factories, the sale of liquor, &c., and the outside world takes no notice. This, however, is a liberty allowed only in towns, and not in villages, the home of conservatism.

With the lower classes the case is different. They are mostly uneducated and have little idea of the religious basis of social usages. These are sanctified by custom, and the Indian peasant is intensely conservative—like Englishmen, of whom Emerson said 'Antiquity of usage is sanction enough. . . . The favourite phrase of their law is "a custom whereof the memory of man runneth not back to the contrary" '. They are not affected by the leaven of western ideas to anything like the same extent as the upper classes, and adopt customs like purdah and the prohibition of widow remarriage in imitation of the upper classes at the very time when an increasing number of the latter are giving them up. While therefore reform is in progress in one section of the community, there is a retrograde movement in another. The remedy must be sought in the general spread of education and the diffusion of enlightenment in the manner portrayed in Lord Macaulay's fine simile: 'The highest intellects, like the tops of the mountains, are the first to catch and to reflect the dawn. They are bright while the level below is still dark. But soon the light, which at first illuminated only the loftiest eminences, descends on the plain and penetrates to the deepest valley.'

The lowest classes are, however, affected by the introduction of the accessories of western civilization such as the train, motor-bus, and factory. When the idea of starting railways was mooted, it was feared that passenger traffic might not pay, as caste considerations might prevent men of high caste sitting in the same carriage as men of low caste. Nothing of the kind has happened. So far from being unpopular, railway travel is extremely popular, though a few punctilious persons consider it necessary to take special precautions against possible pollution. Members of some high castes in the Central Provinces are said to have been so scrupulous that till quite recently they washed the bedding they had taken with them on a railway journey, in order to remove ceremonial, and not material, uncleanliness, and they also used to abstain from food and water while travelling by train. They have now given up these inconvenient customs.[1] Such fastidiousness has in any case been exceptional, and for a long time past prejudices about men of all castes travelling together have been quietly

[1] *Census Report of the Central Provinces and Berar for 1931*, Part I, p. 352.

ignored. There is no doctrine of untouchability in a railway compartment or motor-bus, though a case has been known of untouchable passengers being forced by their fellow passengers to sit on the roof of a motor-bus, and Mr. K. M. Panikkar states that he has seen untouchables refused admission to and forcibly ejected from trains on a State railway in Kathiawar.[1] The industrial system is also indifferent to the niceties of the caste system, and factory hands of different castes work together without any trouble arising.

There are two recent movements of special moment, the woman's movement and that which aims at the uplift of the depressed classes. Both owe much to the peculiar personal influence of Mr. Gandhi. In India, as elsewhere, human nature responds to the impress of personality, and if in addition to the power of personality, a man is believed to have high spiritual qualities, the appeal he makes may prove stronger than custom. Whatever may be thought of Mr. Gandhi's political career, there is no doubt as to the impression he has made on the people of India not only by his call for national regeneration but also because of his simplicity of life, his reputation for asceticism and selflessness, and the spiritual nature of some of his teaching. The title of Mahatma, or the great-souled, which is given to him by the Hindu community is indicative of the reverence in which he is held in spite of what he himself has called his somewhat lowly caste.

Mr. Gandhi has long advocated social reform in such matters as caste, child marriage, and the treatment of women, and has given many proofs of his sincere desire for the uplift of the depressed classes, but none of his declarations has had such a practical far-reaching effect as the fast (alluded to in more detail in Chapter II) which he underwent in 1932 in order to force the Government to agree to his views as to the political representation of the depressed classes. The movement for

[1] *Caste and Democracy* (1933), p. 42.

the amelioration of their lot had been in progress for many
years. Depressed Classes Missions had been established in
different places; seats had been given to their representatives
on the legislatures; their spokesmen were members of the
Round Table Conference. An agitation for their admission
to temples like other Hindus had been in operation for some
time, and Mr. Gandhi had denounced untouchability as a blot
on Hinduism, but the withers of orthodox Hinduism were
unwrung and the majority of Hindus remained apathetic.
His fast, however, broke through their indifference and stirred
them into action—to the surprise, perhaps, of Mr. Gandhi
himself, who had a purely political end in view. Not only were
the depressed classes admitted to many temples which had
hitherto been closed to them, but there has been a salutary
change in the general attitude of a large section of their co-
religionists towards them. Many are giving up the traditional
view, based on the belief in *Karma*, that their condition is due
to the working of the moral law of the universe and that it
would be impious to seek to interfere with that law by measures
for their relief. The view is now advanced that if a man can
be helped, it may be taken as proof that the *karma* from which
he suffered is exhausted, and that to lend him a helping hand
is to act as the agent of his *karma*.

The movement for the emancipation of women also owes
much indirectly to Mr. Gandhi. His call to women to help in
the civil disobedience movement had an extraordinary result,
of which some account has been given in the last chapter with
reference to its effects on the purdah system. Women not
only broke purdah, but also in many cases caste, by doing
nurses' work and by freely eating and drinking together. In
Bombay, women, mostly of high caste, fed 1,000 boycotters
daily and felt it no abasement to cook food, serve it, wash up
the dirty dishes, and scrub floors. Their action marks an
important step forward in the emancipation of women, and

a guess may be hazarded that much as Mr. Gandhi sympa-
thized with their cause,[1] he did not anticipate the repercussions
of his call for their services. His immediate object was to
obtain recruits for his campaign, whose intervention would
make a special appeal to Indian men. The result was almost
a mass movement away from the purdah system.

This is only a late phase of the women's movement, which
has been in progress for many years. At first it sought to
promote women's welfare by means of social and educational
work; a lead in this direction had been given by Christian
Missions, while the Brahmo Samaj in Bengal had already done
much to raise the status of women. Since the introduction of
the Montagu-Chelmsford reforms in 1921 its activities have
extended into the political sphere, the claim of its supporters
being that women should be given a position of political
equality with the women of other countries rather than with
the men of their own. It has had amazingly rapid and easy
success in the political field, and one of its champions has
candidly admitted that women were given political enfran-
chisement almost before they realized that votes were worth
having. 'They have just blown their trumpets once, twice or
thrice, and the walls of Jericho have fallen.'[2] A lady (Mrs.
Reddi) has been Deputy-President of the Madras Legislative
Council and secured the enactment of a measure dealing with
the *devadasi* system, by which girls are dedicated to temples
and consequently in most cases to a life of prostitution.
Another lady has served as a Minister in the Travancore State,

[1] Mr. Gandhi has declared: 'I passionately desire the utmost freedom
for our women. I detest child marriages. I shudder to see a child-widow
and shiver with rage when a husband, just widowed, with brutal indifference contracts another marriage. I deplore the criminal indifference
of parents who keep their daughters utterly ignorant and illiterate and
bring them up only for the purpose of marrying them off to some young
man of means.'

[2] Mrs. R. M. Gray, *Asiatic Review* (1932), p. 560, and *Political India*
(1932), p. 159.

where women have the franchise equally with men and can serve in any public office, and two more have been members of the Round Table Conference.

The movement has so far been taken up by only a small section of the womanhood of India, but that section is an intellectual and decidedly vocal *élite*, and it has behind it a certain power of organization. Two all-India associations have been established—the Women's Indian Association and the National Council of Women in India—besides which there is the All-India Women's Conference on Educational and Social Reform, which by means of discussion and resolutions ventilates the views of the more advanced women, stimulates general interest in questions affecting women, and helps to create public opinion. There has been in consequence a rapid growth not only of political consciousness but of thought on social and economic questions. Practical action has been taken in several directions, such as agitation in favour of raising the age of marriage, which was one of the contributory causes of the enactment of the Child Marriage Restraint Act of 1929. Other questions which are being brought to the front are freedom of choice in marriage, freedom for wives to obtain divorce in certain circumstances, freedom for widows to remarry, and the right of widows and daughters to inherit part of a father's property and so secure some economic independence.

The movement is full of hope for the future; the Simon Commission indeed goes so far as to say that it holds 'the key of progress'. The reason is that social life is largely regulated by women. As is well explained by Mr. J. T. Gwynn:

'The immense power of custom in India is derived from the women. The best-educated Indian has a mother or a wife whose education consists of the Hindu tradition. Whatever his intellect may affirm or deny, it is almost impossible for him to take any course that will hurt the feelings of his womenfolk. When his mother and his wife begin to trust their intellects in preference to Hindu tradition, then the binding force of custom will be broken.'[1]

It is because of the awakening of women themselves which it is likely to bring about that the woman's movement has such great potentialities.

The unobtrusive and valuable work done in this direction by the women's institutes (*mahila samitis*) founded by Mrs. G. S. Dutt (Saroj Nalini) in Bengal shows how receptive of new ideas they can become if their interest is aroused. These institutes have proved the correctness of the view of their foundress that the women of India would respond to efforts for their improvement and that, once they were organized in a co-operative movement, they would become an actively progressive force. In her opinion, no advance could be made in the social sphere without enlisting the senior female members of orthodox Hindu households, with whom real power lies. 'A school for the mothers-in-law', she once said, 'is what we most urgently need in this country.' Women's institutes have proved such a school. Through them women of this class have been brought into touch with new conceptions of life. Hitherto devoted solely to service to their families, they have begun to learn the lesson of service to women outside them, and—a significant sign of development—orthodox Hindu women of the higher classes have begun to attend and take part in meetings in company with men without the screen of the purdah.[2]

There have been such rapid and far-reaching changes in India within the lifetime of the present generation that the phrase 'the unchanging East' is becoming almost a by-word. The changes, it is true, have been mainly political and economic, and those within the social sphere have been far less noticeable. Still society is to some extent adapting itself to

[1] *Indian Politics* (1924), p. 241.
[2] See G. S. Dutt, *A Woman of India* (1929), pp. 96, 105, 139.

modern conditions and is by no means static. As stated in earlier chapters, such institutions of immemorial antiquity as the village community and the joint family are in process of transformation, largely in adaptation to economic changes and in consequence of the growth of individualism. Caste has also been affected though only to a limited extent. The educated classes show a growing impatience with customs which appear to impose unreasonable restraints and to interfere unduly with personal liberty. This is more particularly the case in towns, where there is an increasing liberality of thought and practice. Here the rules as to what may be eaten and drunk, and in what company, are frequently neglected or perfunctorily observed, and traditions as to the age of marriage are often disregarded. An extraordinary exhibition of the spirit of revolt against tradition was seen at Travancore not many years ago, when a great 'intercaste dinner' was held at which 300 high-caste Hindus sat down and ate with as many Indian Christians and a certain number of Moslems and Europeans.

There are some who believe these breaches of caste rules are indicative of, or a prelude to, a break up of the caste system, and even, when taken in conjunction with the decline of the joint family system, the dissolution of the Hindu social organization. But much the same phenomena were observed over a century ago. The great Baptist missionary Ward wrote in 1818 that in numerous instances groups of men belonging to different castes met in secret to eat and smoke together. Many Hindus of the highest as well as of the lowest rank ate meat and other forbidden food. Temptations to promiscuous intercourse with females of all castes were greatly strengthened by the absence of thousands of men from home for months and years together, especially in Calcutta and other large towns, and it was so common for them to cohabit, eat, and smoke with women of other castes that the offence was connived at, especially as it took place at a distance from their relatives.

Looking at these and other breaches of caste rules Ward actually came to the conclusion that the rust of the fetters of the caste system had nearly eaten them through and that the institution of caste must sooner or later fall into utter disuse and contempt.[1]

The wish was perhaps father to the thought, and Ward's hopes may have distorted his judgement. Certain it is that his anticipation of the dissolution of the caste system taking place within any measurable distance of time has been falsified, for caste still maintains a firm hold upon Hindu society, though some of its rules are undoubtedly neglected or broken, more especially by the educated classes in urban centres. Even here, however, society tolerates rather than sanctions laxity, and in the villages, which contain nine-tenths of the population, custom is still strongly entrenched and traditional standards are maintained.

It is true that the authority of the castes in social matters has been weakened to some extent by British rule. The extra-legal punishments imposed by caste tribunals are not recognized by law, and persons aggrieved by them can appeal to the law-courts; in some parts, indeed, the caste councils are nervous about passing sentence in cases brought before them for fear of legal action. Moreover, under the Caste Disabilities Removal Act of 1850, which is in force in British India, loss of caste does not legally involve loss of personal rights, for it expressly lays down that no custom shall be enforceable in a court of law which inflicts forfeiture of rights or of property, or which affects any right of inheritance, as a consequence of loss of caste. The State of Baroda appears to have gone even farther, for, according to reports published in the press, in December 1933, the Maharaja Gaekwar gave his assent to an Act which provides that attempts to inflict

[1] W. Ward, *View of the History, Literature and Mythology of the Hindoos* (Serampore, 1818), pp. xi, xii.

or enforce caste punishments are punishable by a term of
simple imprisonment up to six months or a fine of Rs. 1,000
or both, and, in addition to this, imposes restraints on the
further subdivision of castes and sub-castes.

The equality of all men before the law has done much to
improve the position of the low castes, as they know that they
can obtain legal redress for wrongs, however high the caste of
the wrong-doer. High caste confers no privilege or immunity
in the courts of law, except that in some States Brahmans are
exempt from capital punishment. The rule of equal justice
is not altogether appreciated by the higher castes, if we may
judge from a proverb current in the west of India, which runs:
'The Hindu gods have fled to the hills, the Moslem saints to
Mecca, and low-caste men knock people about.' The traditional view is that if any one is to be knocked about, it should
be the man of low caste; indeed, a popular proverb of Bihar
roundly declares that just as rice should be watered, so the
low castes should be kicked.

Although, however, there is no legal inequality, the social
inequality which is the root principle of the caste system still
persists. Caste regulates social relations; the rules about
eating and drinking limit social intercourse; and the ban on
intermarriage prevents the fusion of different classes into a
homogeneous community.[1]

The movement for the uplift of the depressed classes seems
to hold out some prospect of a reform within the caste system
by removing, or at any rate alleviating, one of its worst abuses.
Within the last few years it has evoked some remarkable
demonstrations of sympathy with their cause, and even of
fellowship with them, which would have been thought incredible twenty years ago. In Travancore, for instance,

---

[1] By an Act passed in 1923 it is legally possible for persons of different
castes to marry, but this involves for a man loss of membership of a joint
family and loss of the right of adoption.

a body of Hindus of good caste went to the Maharaja's palace and petitioned him to allow the untouchables the free use of all public roads. At Munshiganj in Bengal ladies of high caste intervened to secure for the depressed classes the right of entry to a temple. For nine months the depressed classes had vainly endeavoured to secure this right by lying down in front of the shrine day after day and finally by threatening to starve unless and until they were admitted to it. The priests were obdurate, and the impasse was solved by 200 high-caste women, who, sympathizing with their sufferings, broke down the barricades and threw open the doors of the temple.

On the other hand, it has been pointed out that 'the mood of excited benignity' created by Mr. Gandhi's fast did not reach the villages at all, that many demonstrations of sympathy were more theatrical than real, and that a reaction soon set in. 'The truth of the matter is that a system so deeply embedded in the history and traditions of a people, so much a part of their daily lives, is not likely to succumb to a sudden onslaught of emotion.'[1] Reviewing the present position the Census Commissioner for India remarks: 'Though it is conceded that the position of individuals has been much ameliorated as far as public life is concerned, and that untouchability has in that respect been very appreciably reduced, all available information goes to show that in private intercourse, as in religious observances, the castes whose water cannot be accepted are held at as great a distance as before.'[2]

The movement clearly has not yet made much headway among the great mass of the Hindu community. As mentioned in Chapter II, the leader of the depressed classes realizes the scant response made by the Hindu community as a whole to efforts on their behalf. 'Hindu society', he says, 'does not think rationally about its conduct towards the depressed

[1] *India in* 1931–2 (Calcutta, 1933), pp. 64, 65.
[2] *Census for India Report for* 1931, Part I, p. 432.

classes. It leads its customary life and is not prepared to relinquish it even at the bidding of Mr. Gandhi. It refuses to reassess its old values.' Even the depressed classes are not united in their demands. The better educated press for a reform of the caste system and for better social treatment, but others are only anxious to get more material prosperity, to be better fed, better clothed, and better housed. The latter acquiesce in their place under the caste system, which they regard as natural or as part of a divinely ordained order, and are not inclined to kick against the pricks.

Castes which, though ranking above the depressed classes are still of low status, are also pressing for admission to a higher place in the gradation of castes. There is, however, no general demand for the abolition of caste and for the levelling down of the higher castes. What is aimed at by the lower castes is levelling up. So far from advocating any destruction of the social pyramid which the system has built up, they desire merely a higher place in it. Nothing is more noticeable than their anxiety to be recognized as twice-born castes, their assumption in some cases of the sacred thread, which is the outward and visible sign of the twice-born castes, and the increasing solidarity resulting from the formation of caste associations, which seek to better their position by means of organization and agitation as well as by education.

Nor can there be said to be anything like a revolt against the primacy of Brahmans in the hierarchy of castes, though their right to lay down the law in religious and social matters is being questioned in some parts of the country. About sixty years ago a body was founded in Bombay under a name meaning the Society of Purity and Truth, which contests the Brahmans' right to a sacerdotal monopoly, proclaiming that there is no need for intermediaries between the gods and men and that ceremonies can be performed as efficaciously by laymen as by a priestly order. In Madras, again, the political domination of the Brahmans has been shaken by the Justice party, which represents the non-Brahman and stands for justice and equality between all men irrespective of caste, while a branch of the party called 'the self-respect movement' preaches the same doctrine in social matters, and advocates the independence and self-assertion of the non-Brahman.[1]

The general population, however, is unmoved by agitation against the theocratic organization of caste. The very castes which are trying to climb to higher rungs on the social ladder invoke the aid of Brahmans in their efforts to establish their claims. The system is upheld by a great solid mass of public, though not a vocal, opinion. An immense majority of the population is characterized by an ingrained conservatism, an intense reluctance to disturb the existing order of things. There is a new orientation of ideas among the educated classes, but they are only a minority and count for less in the religious and social sphere than in the political sphere; and the masses still cling to their old ways. There are some changes of practice in minor matters, particularly as regards food and occupations, but the main structure of caste remains intact with its mutually exclusive communities, its carefully regulated gradations of rank, and the ban on intermarriage which prevents any fusion of classes: it is as if some superficial cracks had appeared on the stucco front of a building, while the brickwork behind it remained solid. Caste is a complex and highly organized system, the development of many centuries, with which the customs of the people are closely connected and inter-related. In spite of its obvious defects, the artificial barriers which it maintains between classes, the irrational customs which it

[1] There have been similar movements in the past. One was that of the Lingayats mentioned in Chapter I, another that of the Kabirpanthis, a sect founded by Kabir (1380–1420), which inculcated the equality of all men, the abolition of caste, and the worship of one God, requiring neither idols nor temples; but they have so far departed from their principles as to allow of caste distinctions.

sanctions, and the rational practices which it forbids, it is not only the basis of social order, but also in a large measure the source and inspiration of social morality, and its destruction would be a dangerous revolution unless and until its place can be taken by another and a better system.

INDEX